Illustrations of the British Flora: a Series of Wood Engravings, with Dissections, of British Plants

Fitch, W. H. (Walter Hood)

BIBLIOLIFE

ILLUSTRATIONS

OF

THE BRITISH FLORA:

A SERIES OF

WOOD ENGRAVINGS, WITH DISSECTIONS,

OF

British Plants

DRAWN BY

W. H. FITCH, F.L.S.,

AND

W. G. SMITH, F.L.S.

FORMING AN ILLUSTRATED COMPANION TO MR. BENTHAM'S
HANDBOOK AND OTHER BRITISH FLORAS.

Seventh Edition.

LONDON:

LOVELL REEVE & CO., LIMITED,

Publishers to the Home, Colonial, and Indian Governments.

6 HENRIETTA STREET, COVENT GARDEN.

1908.

PREFACE TO THE FIRST EDITION.

THE Illustrated Edition of Mr. Bentham's "Handbook of the British Flora" being exhausted, the wood-engravings of that work are here reproduced as an Illustrated Companion to the "Handbook" and other British Floras. The cuts are arranged according to the last Edition of the "Handbook," and new cuts of the species admitted in recent Editions are added. To facilitate reference from other Floras, where the nomenclature differs from that of the "Handbook," synonyms, in italics, are incorporated in the Index. In this volume and the "Handbook" combined, Students will have, in a more convenient and portable form, all that the Illustrated Edition contained, at little more than one-third the cost.

PREFACE TO THE SECOND EDITION.

THE exhaustion of a large Edition of this work in the course of a few years is a gratifying proof of its utility to, and appreciation by, Students of Botany, and has encouraged the Publishers, in preparing a new Edition for the press, to endeavour to render it still more useful and worthy of the patronage it has already received. In the present Edition five new cuts have been added, and the whole have been rearranged according to the New Edition (the Fifth, just published) of Bentham's "Handbook" as revised by Sir J. D. Hooker. The Index has been greatly enlarged to facilitate reference from other Floras, and a new Index of English and popular names has been added. Lastly, to meet the convenience of Students of limited means, the price of this volume, and also of the Handbook, has been reduced from 12s. to 10s. 6d., the Publishers relying upon an increased sale to compensate them for the surrender thus made. In this volume and the "Handbook" combined, therefore, Students will now have a complete Illustrated British Flora, the best, especially for beginners, for one guinea.

LONDON, *March 22nd, 1887.*

NOTE TO THE THIRD EDITION.

IN this Edition four new cuts have been added, and the whole rearranged in accordance with the newly revised Sixth Edition of the "Handbook."

NATURAL ORDERS

ILLUSTRATED IN THIS VOLUME.

		FIGURES
i.	RANUNCULACEÆ .	1–32
ii.	BERBERIDEÆ . .	33
iii.	NYMPHÆACEÆ .	34, 35
iv.	PAPAVERACEÆ .	36–44
v.	FUMARIACEÆ . .	45–47
vi.	CRUCIFERÆ . .	48–113
vii.	RESEDACEÆ . .	114–116
viii.	CISTACEÆ . . .	117–120
ix.	VIOLACEÆ . . .	121–126
x.	POLYGALACEÆ .	127
xi.	FRANKENIACEÆ .	128
xii.	CARYOPHYLLACEÆ	129–173
xiii.	PORTULACEÆ . .	174, 175
xiv.	TAMARISCINEÆ .	176
xv.	ELATINACEÆ . .	177, 178
xvi.	HYPERICINEÆ .	179–189
xvii.	LINACEÆ . . .	190–194
xviii.	MALVACEÆ . .	195–200
xix.	TILIACEÆ . . .	201
xx.	GERANIACEÆ . .	202–220
xxi.	ACERACEÆ . . .	221, 222
xxii.	AQUIFOLIACEÆ .	223
xxiii.	CELASTRACEÆ . .	224
xxiv.	RHAMNACEÆ . .	225, 226
xxv.	PAPILIONACEÆ .	227–297
xxvi.	ROSACEÆ . . .	298–341

		FIGURES
xxvii.	ONAGRACEÆ . .	342–354
xxviii.	LYTHRARIEÆ . .	355–357
xxix.	CUCURBITACEÆ .	358
xxx.	CRASSULACEÆ .	359–371
xxxi.	RIBESIACEÆ . .	372–375
xxxii.	SAXIFRAGACEÆ .	376–391
xxxiii.	DROSERACEÆ . .	392–394
xxxiv.	HALORAGEÆ . .	395–397
xxxv.	UMBELLIFERÆ .	398–456
xxxvi.	ARALIACEÆ . .	457
xxxvii.	LORANTHACEÆ .	458
xxxviii.	CORNACEÆ . . .	459, 460
xxxix.	CAPRIFOLIACEÆ .	461–469
xl.	STELLATÆ . . .	470–483
xli.	VALERIANEÆ . .	484–491
xlii.	DIPSACEÆ . . .	492–496
xliii.	COMPOSITÆ . .	497–611
xliv.	CAMPANULACEÆ .	612–625
xlv.	ERICACEÆ . . .	626–648
xlvi.	PRIMULACEÆ . .	649–663
xlvii.	LENTIBULACEÆ .	664–669
xlviii.	OLEACEÆ . . .	670, 671
xlix.	APOCYNACEÆ . .	672, 673
l.	GENTIANACEÆ .	674–684
li.	POLEMONIACEÆ .	685
lii.	CONVOLVULACEÆ.	686–691

	FIGURES
liii BORAGINEÆ . .	692–712
liv. SOLANACEÆ . .	713–717
lv. OROBANCHACEÆ .	718–725
lvi. SCROPHULARINEÆ	726–776
lvii. LABIATÆ . . .	777–821
lviii. VERBENACEÆ. .	822
lix. PLUMBAGINEÆ .	823–827
lx. PLANTAGINEÆ .	828–833
lxi. ILLECEBRACEÆ .	834–838
lxii. CHENOPODIACEÆ	839–857
lxiii. POLYGONACEÆ .	858–879
lxiv. THYMELEACEÆ .	880, 881
lxv. ELÆAGNACEÆ .	882
lxvi. SANTALACEÆ. .	883
lxvii ARISTOLOCHIACEÆ	884
lxviii. EUPHORBIACEÆ .	885–899
lxix. EMPETRACEÆ .	900
lxx CALLITRICHINEÆ	901, 902
lxxi. URTICACEÆ . .	903–907
lxxii ULMACEÆ . . .	908, 909
lxxiii. AMENTACEÆ . .	910–935
lxxiv. CONIFERÆ. . .	936–938

	FIGURES
lxxv. TYPHACEÆ .	939–943
lxxvi. AROIDEÆ .	944, 945
lxxvii. LEMNACEÆ .	946–950
lxxviii. NAIADEÆ . .	951–971
lxxix. ALISMACEÆ .	972–977
lxxx. HYDROCHA-RIDEÆ . .	978–980
lxxxi. ORCHIDACEÆ .	981–1016
lxxxii. IRIDEÆ . . .	1017–1023
lxxxiii. AMARYLLIDEÆ	1024–1027
lxxxiv. DIOSCORIDEÆ.	1028
lxxxv. LILIACEÆ . .	1029–1059
lxxxvi. JUNCACEÆ. .	1060–1081
lxxxvii. ERIOCAULEÆ .	1082
lxxxviii. CYPERACEÆ .	1083–1157
lxxxix. GRAMINEÆ. .	1158–1258
xc. LYCOPODIACEÆ	1259–1263
xci. SELAGINEL-LACEÆ . .	1264–1266
xcii. MARSILEACEÆ	1267
xciii. EQUISETACEÆ	1268–1277
xciv. FILICES. . .	1278–1315

ILLUSTRATIONS

OF THE

BRITISH FLORA

RANUNCULACEÆ.

1. Clematis Vitalba.

2. Thalictrum alpinum.

3. Thalictrum minus.

4. Thalictrum flavum.

A

5. Anemone Pulsatilla.

6. Anemone nemorosa.

7. Adonis autumnalis.

8. Myosurus minimus.

9. Ranunculus aquatilis.

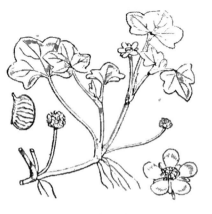

10. Ranunculus hederaceus.

11. Ranunculus Lingua.   12. Ranunculus Flammula.

13. Ranunculus ophioglossifolius]   15. Ranunculus sceleratus.

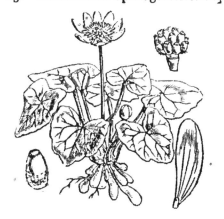

14. Ranunculus Ficaria.   16. Ranunculus auricomus.

18.   Ranunculus repens.

17.   Ranunculus acris.

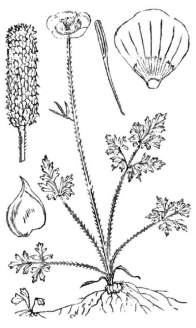

20.   Ranunculus bulbosus.

19.   Ranunculus flabellatus.

21.   Ranunculus hirsutus.

22.   Ranunculus parviflorus.

23. Ranunculus arvensis.

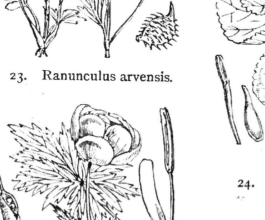

24. Caltha palustris.

25. Trollius europæus.

26. Helleborus viridis.

27. Helleborus fœtidus.

28. Aquilegia vulgaris,   29.   Delphinium Ajacis.

30, Aconitum Napellus.   31.   Actæa spicata.

32. Pæonia officinalis.

33. Berberis vulgaris.

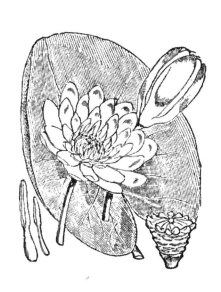

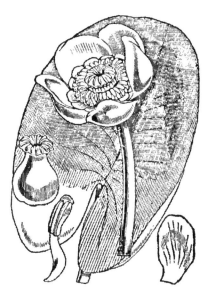

34. Nymphæa alba.

35. Nuphar luteum.

36. Papaver somniferum.

37. Papaver Rhœas.

38. Papaver dubium.

39. Papaver hybridum.

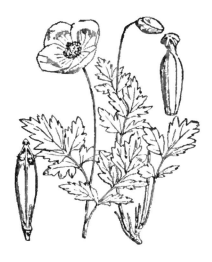

40. Papaver Argemone.

41. Meconopsis cambrica.

42. Chelidonium majus.

43. Rœmeria hybrida.

46.   Corydalis lutea.

44.   Glaucium luteum.

47.   Corydalis claviculata.

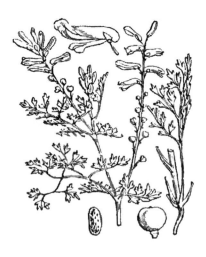

45.   Fumaria officinalis.

48.   Matthiola incana.

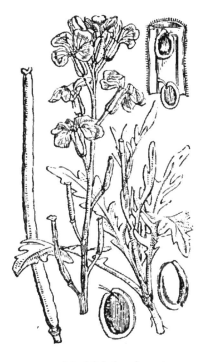

49. Matthiola sinuata.

51. Barbarea vulgaris.

50. Cheiranthus Cheiri.

52. Nasturtium officinale.

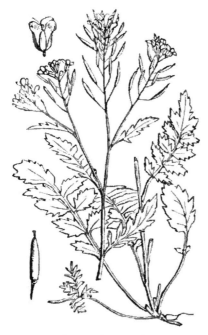

53. Nasturtium sylvestre.

54. Nasturtium palustre.

55. Nasturtium amphibium.

56. Arabis perfoliata.

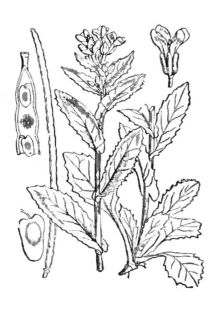

57. Arabis Turrita.

59. Arabis alpina.

58. Arabis hirsuta.

60. Arabis ciliata.

61. Arabis Thaliana.

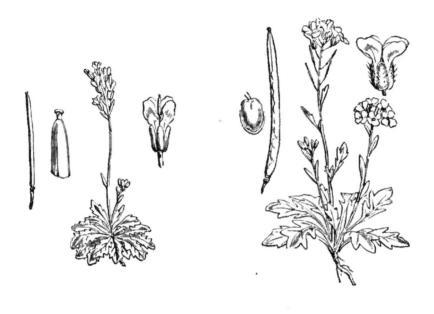

62. Arabis stricta.　　　　63. Arabis petræa.

64. Cardamine amara.　　　　65. Cardamine pratensis.

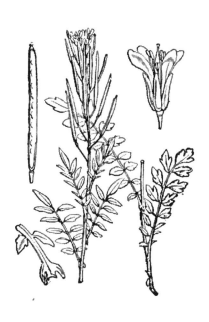

66. Cardamine impatiens.

67. Cardamine hirsuta.

68. Cardamine bulbifera.

69. Hesperis matronalis.

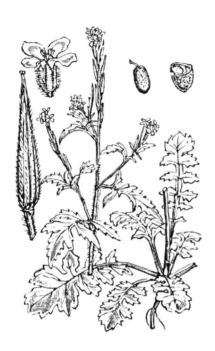

70. Sisymbrium officinale.

71. Sisymbrium Irio.

72. Sisymbrium Sophia.

73. Alliaria officinalis.

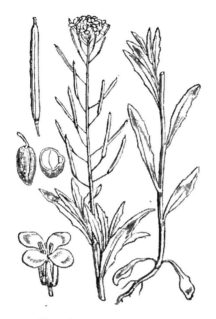

74. Erysimum cheiranthoides.

75. Erysimum orientale.

76. Brassica tenuifolia.

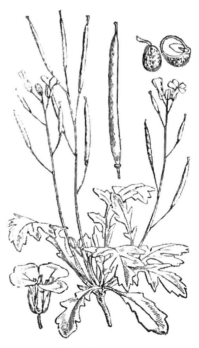

77. Brassica muralis.

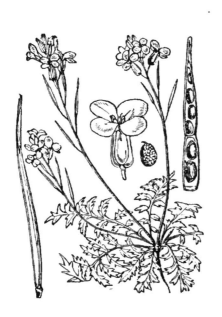

78. Brassica monensis.   79. Brassica oleracea.

80. Brassica campestris.   81. Brassica alba.

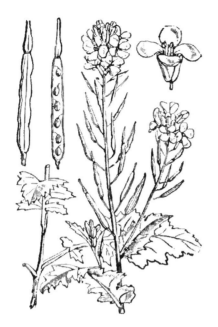

82. **Brassica Sinapis.**

83. **Brassica nigra.**

84. **Brassica adpressa.**

85. **Cochlearia armoracia.**

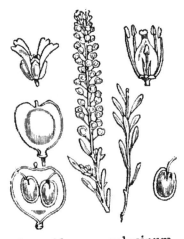

87. **Alyssum calycinum.**

86. **Cochlearia officinalis.**

89. **Draba aizoides.**

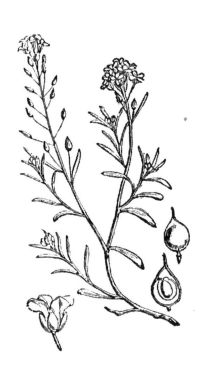

88. **Alyssum maritimum.**

90. **Draba hirta.**

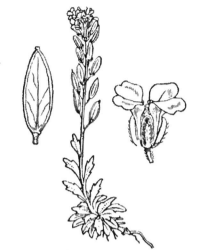

91.   Draba incana.

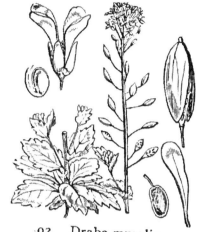

92.   Draba muralis.

93.   Draba verna.

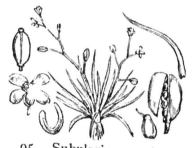

95.   Subularia aquatica.

94.   Camelina sativa.

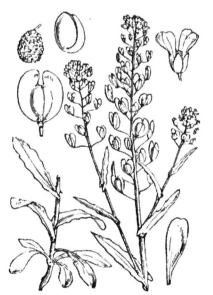

96.   Thlaspi arvense.

99.   Teesdalia nudicaulis.

97.   Thlaspi perfoliatum.

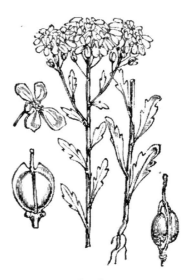

100.   Iberis amara.

98.   Thlaspi alpestre.

101.   Hutchinsia petræa.

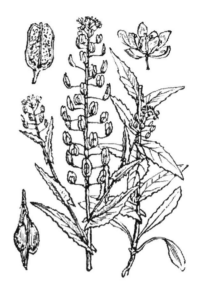

102. Capsella Bursa-pastoris.

103. Lepidium campestre.

104. Lepidium Smithii.

105. Lepidium Draba.

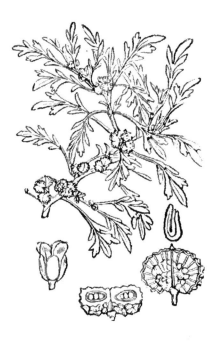

106. Lepidium latifolium.

108. Senebiera Coronopus.

107. Lepidium ruderale.

109. Senebiera didyma.

110.   Isatis tinctoria.

112.   Crambe maritima.

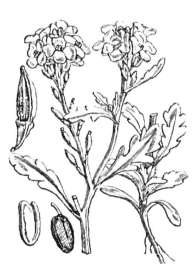

111.   Cakile maritima.

113.   Raphanus Raphanistrum.

114.　Reseda luteola.

115.　Reseda lutea.

116.　Reseda alba.

117.　Helianthemum guttatum.

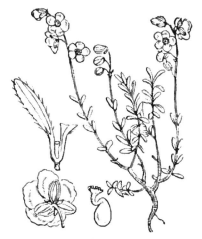

118. Helianthemum canum.

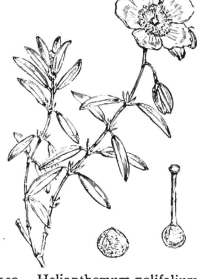

120. Helianthemum polifolium.

119. Helianthemum vulgare.

121. Viola palustris.

122. Viola odorata.

123. Viola hirta.

124.   Viola arenaria.

125.   Viola canina.

126.   Viola tricolor.

127.   Polygala vulgaris.

129.   Dianthus prolifer.

128   Frankenia lævis.

130. **Dianthus Armeria.**

131. Dianthu deltoides.

132. Dianthus cæsius.

133. Saponaria officinalis.

134. Silene acaulis.

135.   Silene Cucubalus.   136.   Silene Otites.

137.   Silene nutans.   138.   Silene gallica.

139. Silene conica.

140. Silene noctiflora.

141. Lychnis vespertina.

142. Lychnis diurna.

143.　Lychnis Githago.

144.　Lychnis Flos-cuculi.

145.　Lychnis Viscaria.

146.　Lychnis alpina.

147.   Sagina procumbens.

148.   Sagina Linnæi.

149.   Sagina nodosa.

150.   Arenaria Cherleri.

C

151.   Arenaria verna.

152.   Arenaria uliginosa.

153.   Arenaria tenuifolia.

154.   Arenaria peploides.

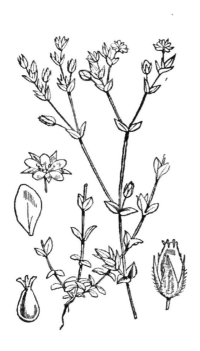

155. Arenaria serpyllifolia.

157. Arenaria trinervis.

156. Arenaria ciliata.

158. Mœnchia erecta.

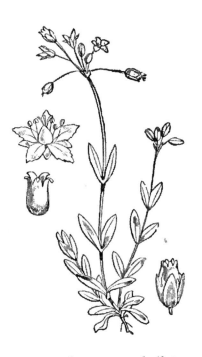

159.   Holosteum umbellatum.

161.   Cerastium arvense.

162.   Cerastium alpinum.

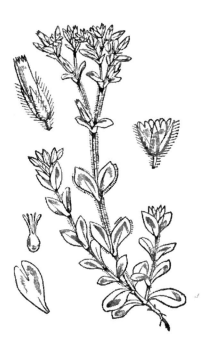

160.   Cerastium vulgatum.

163.   Cerastium trigynum.

164. Stellaria aquatica.

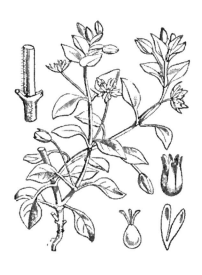

166. Stellaria media.

165. Stellaria nemorum.

167. Stellaria uliginosa.

168. Stellaria graminea.

169. Stellaria palustris.

170. Stellaria Holostea.

171. Spergularia rubra.

172. Spergula arvensis.

173. Polycarpon tetraphyllum.

174. Claytonia perfoliata.

176. Tamarix gallica.

175. Montia fontana.

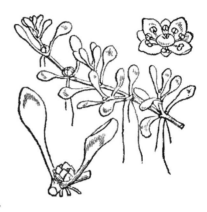

177.   Elatine hexandra.   178.   Elatine Hydropiper.

179.   Hypericum calycinum.   180.   Hypericum Androsæmum.

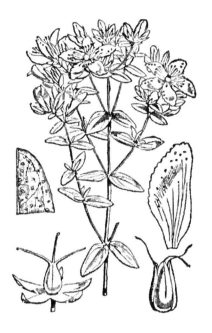

181. Hypericum perforatum.   182. Hypericum dubium.

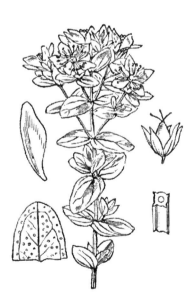

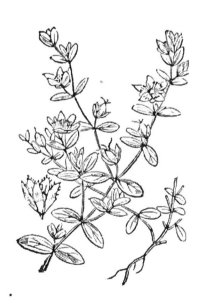

183. Hypericum quadrangulum.   184. Hypericum humifusum.

185.   Hypericum linarifolium.

187.   Hypericum hirsutum.

186.   Hypericum pulchrum.

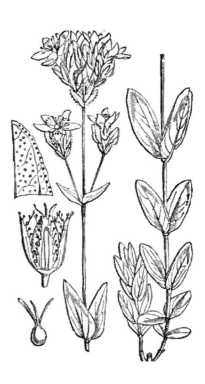

188.   Hypericum montanum,

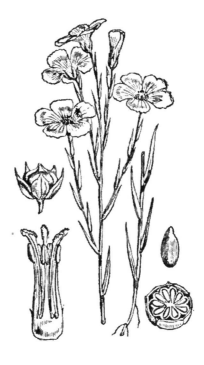

189. Hypericum Elodes.

190. Linum usitatissimum.

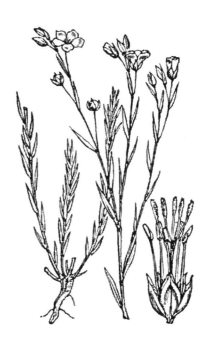

191. Linum perenne.

192. Linum angustifolium.

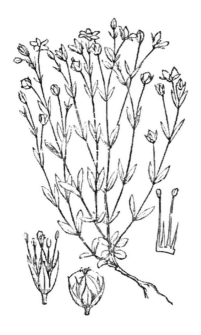

193. Linum catharticum.   194. Radiola Millegrana.

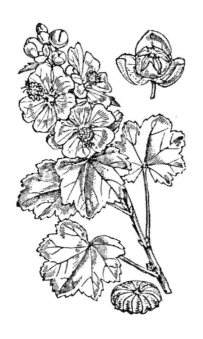

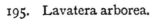

195. Lavatera arborea.   196. Malva rotundifolia.

197. Malva sylvestris.

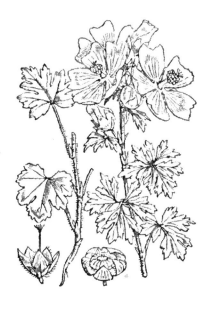

198. Malva moschata.

199. Althæa officinalis.

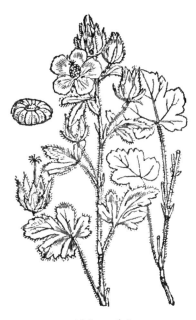

200. Althæa hirsuta.

201. Tilia europæa.   202. Geranium sanguineum.

203. Geranium phæum.   204. Geranium sylvaticum.

205. Geranium pratense.

206. Geranium pyrenaicum.

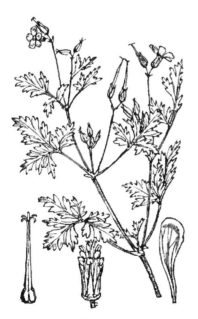

207. Geranium Robertianum.

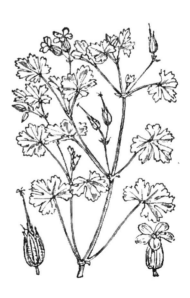

208. Geranium lucidum.

209. Geranium molle.

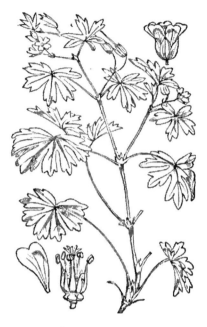

210. Geranium pusillum.

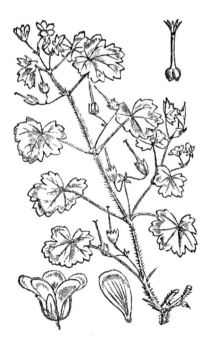

211. Geranium rotundifolium.

212. Geranium dissectum.

213. Geranium columbinum.

215. Erodium moschatum.

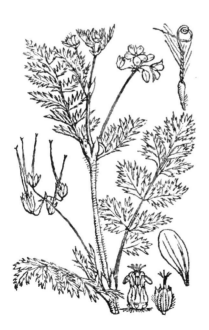

214. Erodium cicutarium.

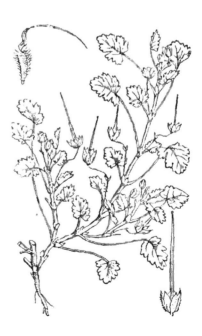

216. Erodium maritimum.

 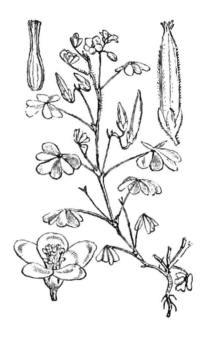

217.   Oxalis Acetosella.   218.   Oxalis corniculata.

219.   Impatiens Noli-me-tangere.   220.   Impatiens fulva.

221. Acer campestre.

222. Acer Pseudo-platanus.

223. Ilex Aquifolium.

224. Evonymus europæus.

225. Rhamnus catharticus. 226. Rhamnus Frangula.

227. Ulex europæus   228. Ulex nanus.

229. Genista tinctoria.

230. Genista pilosa.

231. Genista anglica.

232. Cytisus scoparius.

233. Ononis arvensis.   234. Ononis reclinata.

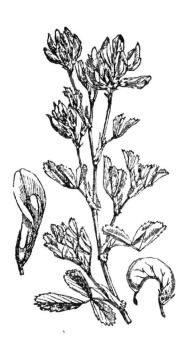

235. Medicago falcata.   236. Medicago sativa.

237. Medicago lupulina.

238. Medicago denticulata.

239. Medicago maculata.

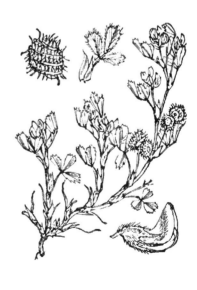

240. Medicago minima.

241.   Melilotus officinalis.

242.   Melilotus arvensis.

243.   Melilotus alba

244.   Trigonella purpurascens.

245. Trifolium incarnatum.

246. Trifolium arvense.

247. Trifolium stellatum.

248. Trifolium ochroleucum.

249.   Trifolium pratense.

250.   Trifolium medium.

251.   Trifolium maritimum.

252.   Trifolium striatum.

253. Trifolium Bocconi.

254. Trifolium scabrum.

255. Trifolium strictum.

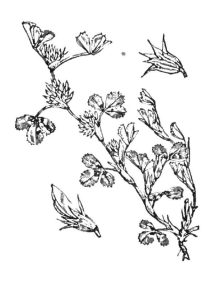

256. Trifolium glomeratum.

257. Trifolium suffocatum.

258. Trifolium resupinatum.   259. Trifolium subterraneum.

260. Trifolium fragiferum.   261. Trifolium repens.

262. Trifolium hybridum.   263. Trifolium procumbens.

264. Trifolium minus.   265. Trifolium filiforme.

266.   Lotus corniculatus.   267.   Lotus angustissimus.

268.   Anthyllis Vulneraria.   269.   Astragalus danicus.

270. Astragalus alpinus.

271. Astragalus glycyphyllos.

272. Oxytropis campestris.

273. Oxytropis uralensis.

274. Ornithopus ebracteatus.

275. Ornithopus perpusillus.

276. Hippocrepis comosa.

277. Onobrychis sativa.

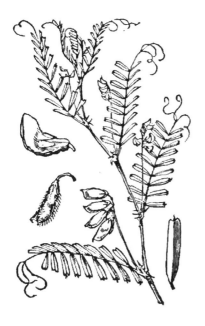

278. Vicia hirsuta.

279. Vicia tetrasperma.

280. Vicia Cracca.

281. Vicia sylvatica.

E

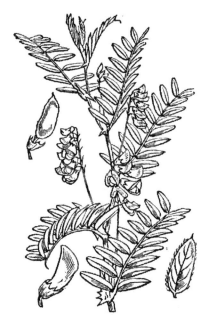

282.   Vicia Orobus.

283.   Vicia sepium.

284.   Vicia lutea.

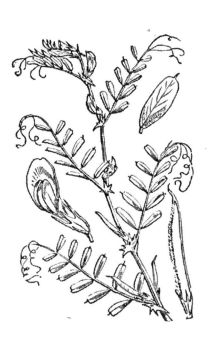

285.   Vicia sativa.

286.   Vicia lathyroides.

287.   Vicia bithynica.

288.   Lathyrus Nissolia.

289.   Lathyrus Aphaca.

290. Lathyrus hirsutus.

291. Lathyrus pratensis.

292. Lathyrus tuberosus.

293. Lathyrus sylvestris.

294. Lathyrus palustris.

295. Lathyrus maritimus.

296. Lathyrus macrorrhizus.

297. Lathyrus niger.

298.   Prunus spinosa.   299.   Prunus Cerasus.

300.   Prunus Padus.   301.   Spiræa salicifolia.

302. Spiræa Ulmaria.

303. Spiræa Filipendula.

304. Dryas octopetala.

305. Geum urbanum.

306. Geum rivale.

307. Rubus Idæus.

308. Rubus fruticosus,

309. Rubus cæsius.

310. Rubus saxatilis.

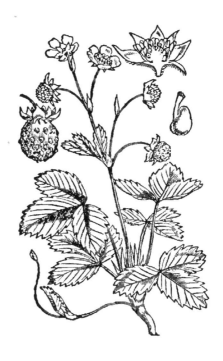

312. Fragaria vesca.

311. Rubus Chamæmorus.

313. Potentilla Fragariastrum.

314. Potentilla reptans.

315. Potentilla Tormentilla.

316. Potentilla argentea.

317. Potentilla verna.

318.   Potentilla Sibbaldi.

319.   Potentilla fruticosa.

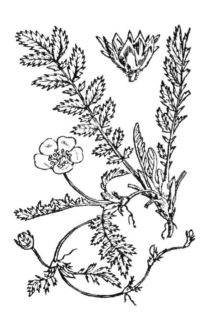

320.   Potentilla anserina.

321.   Potentilla rupestris.

322.　**Potentilla palustris.**　　323.　**Alchemilla vulgaris.**

324.　**Alchemilla alpina.**　　325.　**Alchemilla arvensis.**

326. Sanguisorba officinalis.

327. Poterium Sanguisorba.

328. Agrimonia Eupatoria.

329. Rosa pimpinellifolia.

330. Rosa villosa.

331. Rosa rubiginosa.

332. Rosa canina.

333. Rosa arvensis.

334. Pyrus communis.

335. Pyrus Malus.

336. Pyrus Aria.

337. Pyrus torminalis.

338. Pyrus Aucuparia.

339. Cratægus Oxyacantha.

340. Cotoneaster vulgaris.

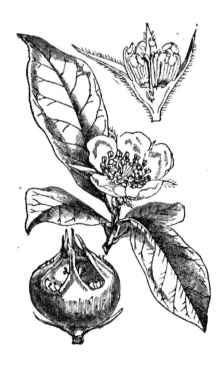

341. Mespilus germanica.

342. Epilobium angustifolium.

343. Epilobium hirsutum.

344. Epilobium parviflorum.

345. Epilobium montanum.

F

346. **Epilobium roseum.**

347. **Epilobium tetragonum.**

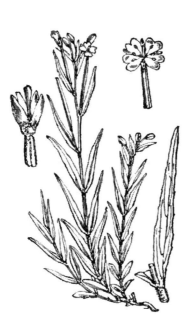

348. **Epilobium palustre.**

349. **Epilobium alsinefolium.**

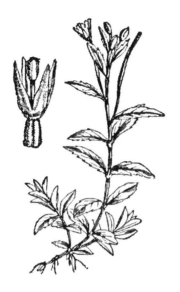

350. Epilobium alpinum.

352. Ludwigia palustris.

351. Œnothera biennis.

353. Circæa lutetiana.

354. Circæa alpina.

355. Lythrum Salicaria.

356. Lythrum hyssopifolium.

357. Peplis Portula.

358. Bryonia dioica.

359. Tillæa muscosa.

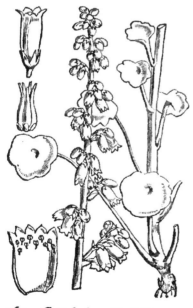

360. Cotyledon Umbilicus.

361. Sedum Rhodiola.

362. Sedum Telephium.

363.   Sedum anglicum.

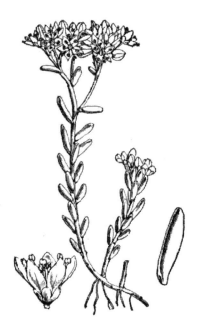

365.   Sedum album.

364.   Sedum dasyphyllum.

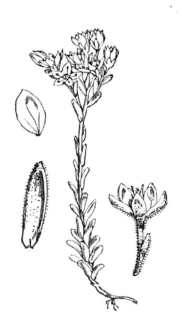

367.   Sedum acre.   366.   Sedum villosum.

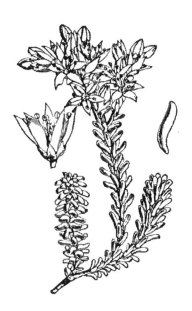

368. Sedum sexangulare.

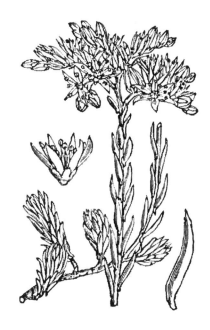

369. Sedum rupestre.

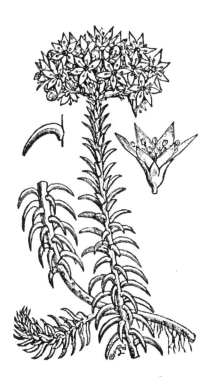

370. Sedum reflexum.

371. Sempervivum tectorum.

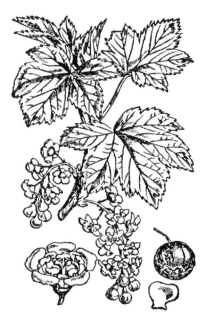

372.   Ribes Grossularia.   373.   Ribes rubrum.

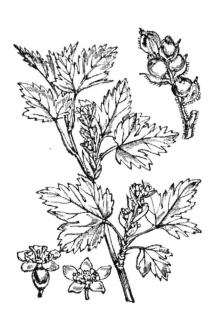

374.   Ribes alpinum.   375.   Ribes nigrum.

376. Saxifraga oppositifolia. 377. Saxifraga aizoides.

378. Saxifraga Hirculus. 379. Saxifraga hypnoides,

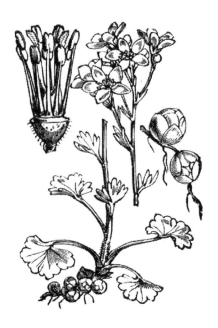

380. Saxifraga cæspitosa.

381. Saxifraga granulata.

382. Saxifraga cernua.

383. Saxifraga rivularis.

384. Saxifraga tridactylites.

385. Saxifraga nivalis.

386. Saxifraga stellaris.

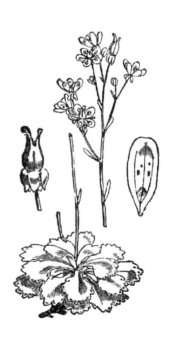

387. Saxifraga umbrosa.

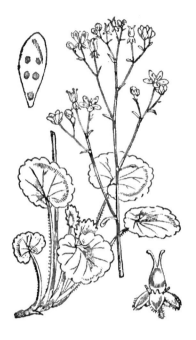

388.   Saxifraga Geum.

389.   Chrysosplenium oppo-
sitifolium.

390.   Chrysosplenium alternifolium.

391.   Parnassia palustris.

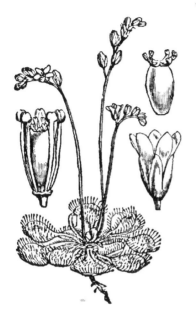

392. Drosera rotundifolia.

393. Drosera longifolia.

394. Drosera anglica.

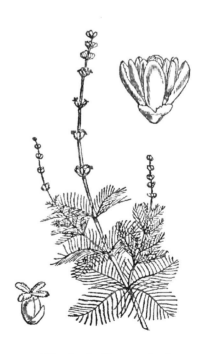

395. Myriophyllum spicatum.

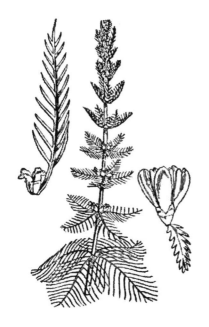

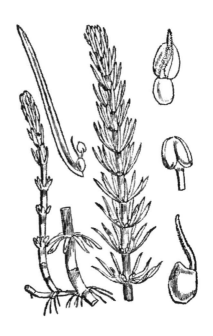

396. **Myriophyllum verticillatum.**

397. **Hippuris vulgaris.**

398. **Hydrocotyle vulgaris.**

399. **Sanicula europæa.**

400. Astrantia major.

401. Eryngium maritimum.

402. Eryngium campestre.

403. Cicuta virosa.

404. Apium graveolens.

405. Apium nodiflorum.

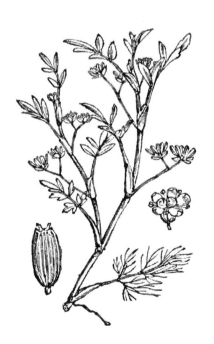

406. Apium inundatum.

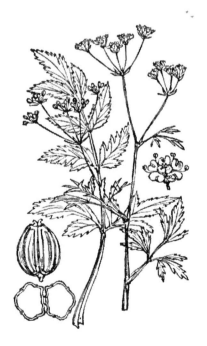

407. Sison Amomum.

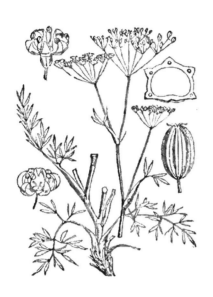

408. Trinia vulgaris.

409. Ægopodium Podagraria.

410. Carum Petroselinum.

411. Carum segetum.

412.   Carum verticillatum.

413.   Carum Carvi.

414.   Carum Bulbocastanum.

415.   Sium latifolium.

416. Sium angustifolium.

417. Pimpinella Saxifraga.

418. Pimpinella magna.

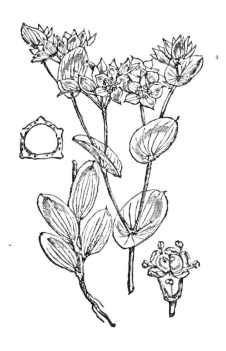

419. Bupleurum rotundifolium.

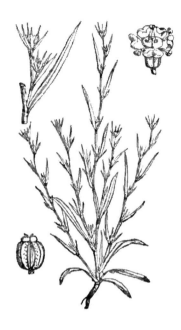

420.   Bupleurum aristatum.   421.   Bupleurum tenuissimum.

422.   Bupleurum falcatum.   423.   Œnanthe fistulosa.

424. Œnanthe pimpinelloides.

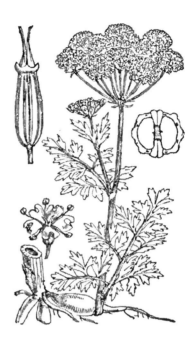

425. Œnanthe crocata.

426. Œnanthe Phellandrium.

427. Æthusa Cynapium.

428. Fœniculum vulgare.

429. Seseli Libanotis.

430. Ligusticum scoticum.

431. Silaus pratensis.

432. Meum athamanticum.

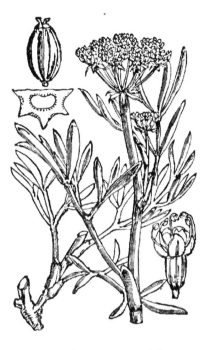

433. Chrithmum maritimum.

434. Angelica sylvestris.

435. Peucedanum officinale.

436. Peucedanum palustre.   437. Peucedanum Ostruthium.

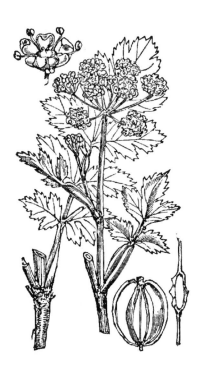

438. Pastinaca sativa.   439. Heracleum Sphondylium.

440. Tordylium maximum.

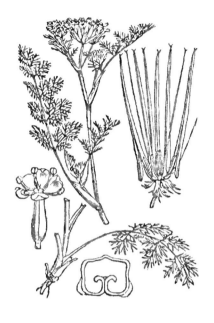

441. Scandix Pecten.

442. Myrrhis odorata.

443. Conopodium denudatum.

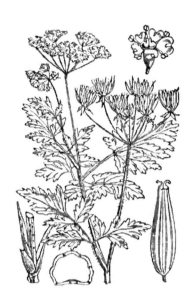

444.   Chærophyllum temulum.

445.   Chærophyllum sylvestre.

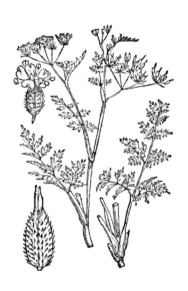

446.   Chærophyllum Anthriscus.

447.   Caucalis nodosa.

448. Caucalis Anthriscus.

449. Caucalis arvensis.

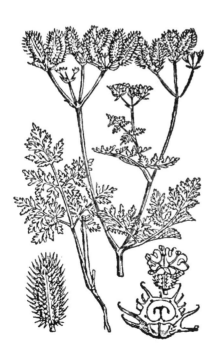

450. Caucalis daucoides.

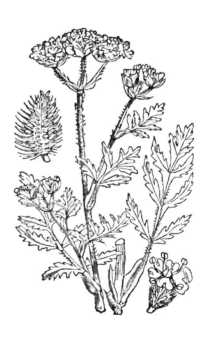

451. Caucalis latifolia.

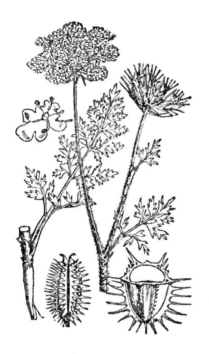

452. Daucus Carota.

453. Conium maculatum.

454. Physospermum cornubiense.

455. Smyrnium Olusatrum.

456. Coriandrum sativum.

457. Hedera Helix.

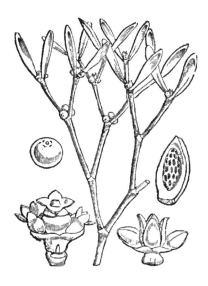

458. Viscum album.

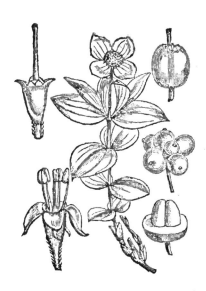

459. Cornus suecica.

460. Cornus sanguinea.   461. Adoxa Moschatellina.

462. Sambucus nigra.   463. Sambucus Ebulus.

464. Viburnum Lantana.

465. Viburnum Opulus.

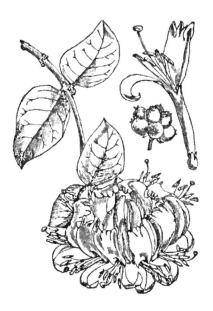

466. Lonicera Periclymenum.

467. Lonicera Caprifolium.

468.   Lonicera Xylosteum.   469.   Linnæa borealis.

470.   Rubia peregrina.   471.   Galium Cruciata.

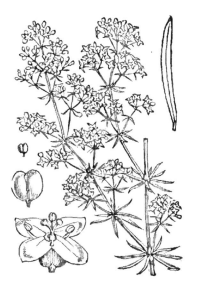

472. Galium verum.

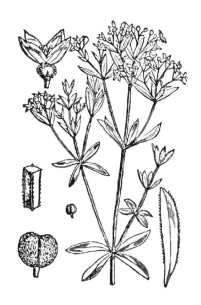

473. Galium palustre.

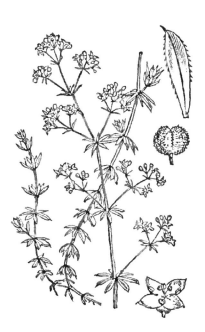

474. Galium uliginosum.

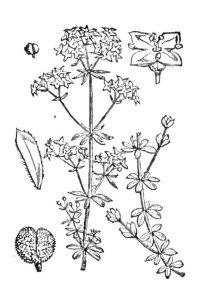

475. Galium saxatile.

H

476.　Galium Mollugo.

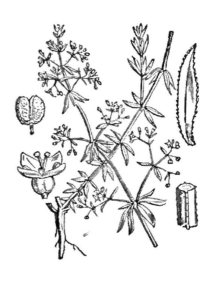

477.　Galium anglicum.

478.　Galium boreale.

479.　Galium Aparine.

480.　Galium tricorne.

481.　Asperula odorata.

482.　Asperula cynanchica.

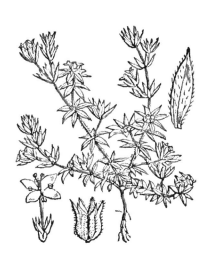

483.　Sherardia arvensis.

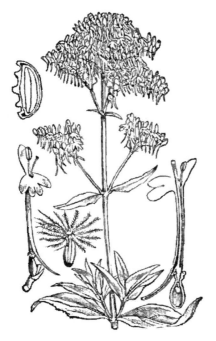

484. Centranthus ruber.

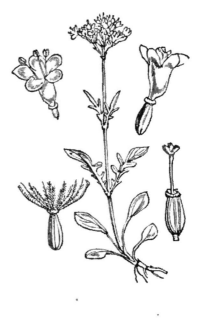

485. Valeriana dioica.

486. Valeriana officinalis.

487. Valeriana pyrenaica.

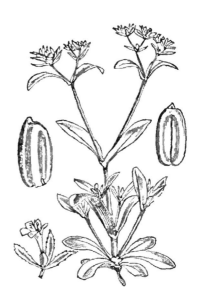

488. Valerianella olitoria.

489. Valerianella carinata.

490. Valerianella Auricula.

491. Valerianella dentata.

492. Dipsacus sylvestris.

493. Dipsacus pilosus.

494. Scabiosa succisa.

495. Scabiosa Columbaria.

496. Scabiosa arvensis.

497. Eupatorium cannabinum.

498. Aster Tripolium.

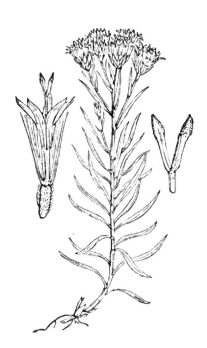

499. Aster Linosyris.

500.   Erigeron acris.   501.   Erigeron alpinus.

502.   Erigeron canadensis.   503.   Solidaga Virga-aurea.

504. Bellis perennis.

505. Filago Germanica.

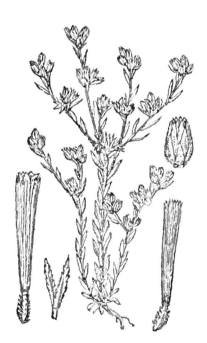

506. Filago minima.

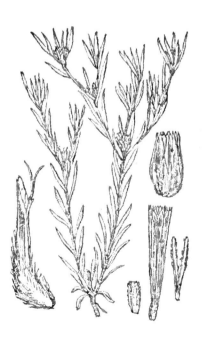

507. Filago gallica.

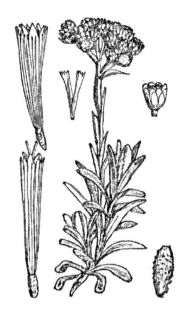

508. Gnaphalium luteo-album.   509. Gnaphalium sylvaticum.

510. Gnaphalium supinum.   511. Gnaphalium uliginosum.

512.   Antennaria dioica.

513.   Antennaria margaritacea.

514.   Inula Helenium.

515.   Inula salicina.

516.   Inula crithmoides.

517.   Inula Conyza.

518.   Inula dysenterica.

519.   Inula Pulicaria.

520.   Xanthium Strumarium.

521.   Bidens cernua.

522.   Bidens tripartita.

523. Chrysanthemum Leucan-
themum.

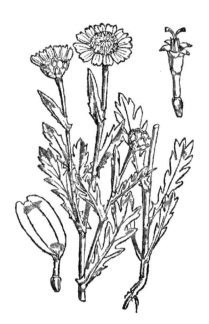 

524. Chrysanthemum segetum.   525. Chrysanthemum Parthenium.

526.   Matricaria inodora.   527.   Matricaria Chamomilla.

528. Anthemis Cotula.

529. Anthemis arvensis.

530. Anthemis nobilis.

531. Anthemis tinctoria.

532. Achillea Ptarmica.

533. Achillea Millefolium.

534. Diotis maritima.

535. Tanacetum vulgare.

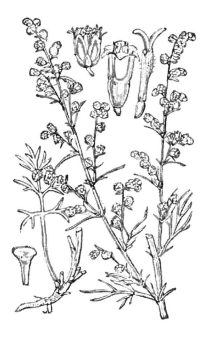

536. Artemisia campestris.

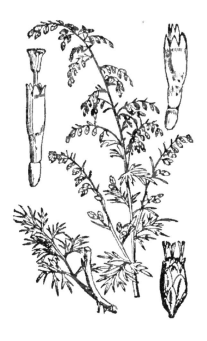

537. Artemisia maritima.

538. Artemisia vulgaris.

539. Artemisia Absinthium.

540.   Tussilago Farfara.   541.   Tussilago Petasites.

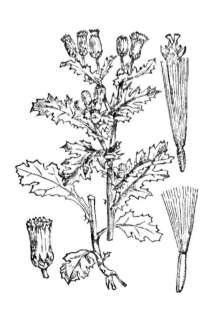

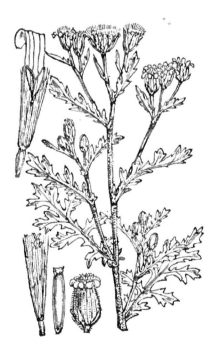

542.   Senecio vulgaris.   543.   Senecio viscosus.

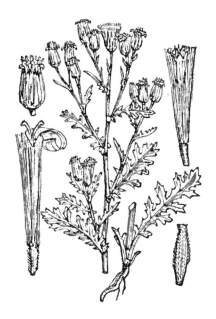

544. Senecio sylvaticus.

545. Senecio squalidus.

546. Senecio aquaticus.

547. Senecio Jacobæa.

548.   Senecio erucifolius.

549.   Senecio paludosus.

550.   Senecio saracenicus.

551.   Senecio palustris.

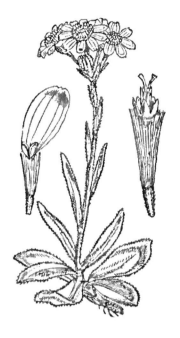

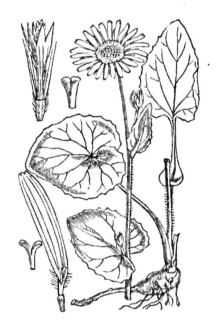

552. Senecio campestris.   553. Doronicum Pardalianches.

554. Doronicum plantagineum.   555. Arctium Lappa.

556.   Serratula tinctoria.   557.   Saussurea alpina.

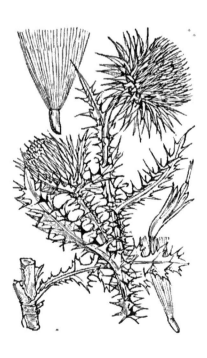

558.   Carduus Marianus.   559.   Carduus nutans.

560. Carduus acanthoides.

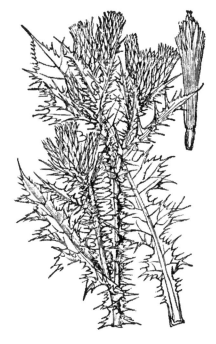

561. Carduus pycnocephalus.

562. Carduus lanceolatus.

563. Carduus palustris.

564. Carduus arvensis.   565. Carduus eriophorus.

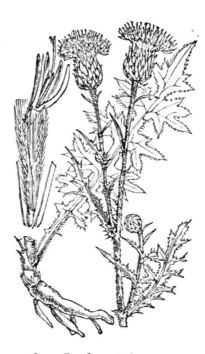

566. Carduus heterophyllus.   567. Carduus tuberosus.

568. Carduus pratensis.

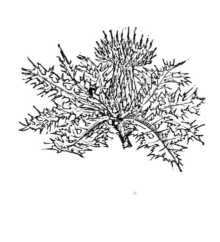

569. Carduus acaulis.

570. Onopordon Acanthium.

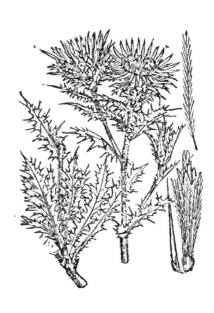

571. Carlina vulgaris.

572. Centaurea nigra.

573. Centaurea Scabiosa.

574. Centaurea Cyanus.

575. Centaurea aspera.

576. Centaurea Calcitrapa.

577. Centaurea solstitialis.

578. Tragopogon pratensis.

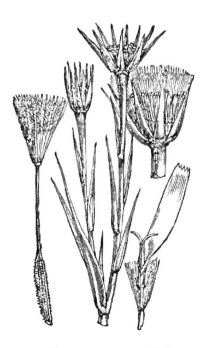

579. Tragopogon porrifolius.

580. Helminthia echioides.   581. Picris hieracioides.

582. Leontodon hispidus.   583. Leontodon autumnalis.

584. Leontodon hirtus.

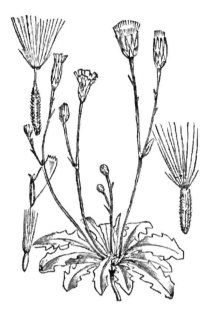

585. Hypochœris glabra.

586. Hypochœris radicata.

587. Hypochœris maculata.

588.　Lactuca muralis.

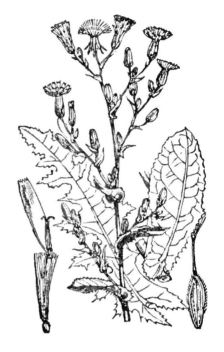

589.　Lactuca Scariola.

590.　Lactuca saligna.

591.　Lactuca alpina.

592. Sonchus arvensis.

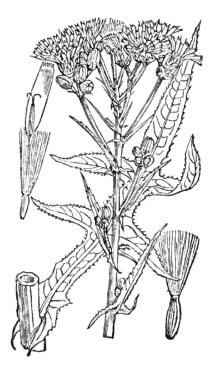

593. Sonchus palustris.

594. Sonchus oleraceus.

595. Taraxacum Dens-leonis.

596. Crepis taraxacifolia.

597. Crepis fœtida.

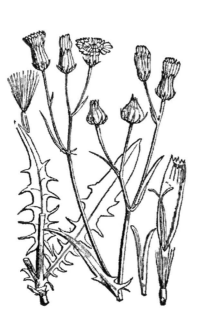

598. Crepis virens.

599. Crepis biennis.

600.   Crepis hieracioides.

601.   Crepis paludosa.

602.   Hieracium Pilosella.

603.   Hieracium alpinum.

604. Hieracium murorum.

605. Hieracium cerinthoides.

606. Hieracium umbellatum.

607. Hieracium sabaudum.

608. Hieracium prenanthoides.

609. Cichorium Intybus.

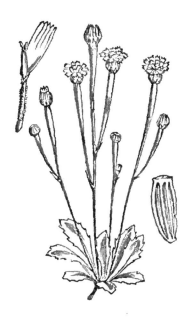

610. Arnoseris pusilla.

611. Lapsana communis.

612. Lobelia Dortmanna.　　613. Lobelia urens.

614. Jasione montana.　　615. Phyteuma orbiculare.

616. Phyteuma spicatum.

617. Campanula glomerata.

618. Campanula Trachelium.

619. Campanula latifolia.

620. Campanula rapunculoides.

621. Campanula Rapunculus.

622. Campanula patula.

623. Campanula rotundifolia.

624. Campanula hederacea.

625. Campanula hybrida.

626. Vaccinium Myrtillus.

627. Vaccinium uliginosum.

628. Vaccinium Vitis-idæa.   629. Vaccinium Oxycoccos.

630. Arbutus Unedo.   631. Arctostaphylos Uva-ursi.

632. Arctostaphylos alpina.

634. Loiseleuria procumbens.

633. Andromeda polifolia.

635. Menziesia polifolia.

640. Erica carnea.

641. Erica vagans.

642. Calluna vulgaris.

643. Pyrola uniflora.

644. Pyrola rotundifolia.

645. Pyrola media.

646. Pyrola minor.

647. Pyrola secunda.

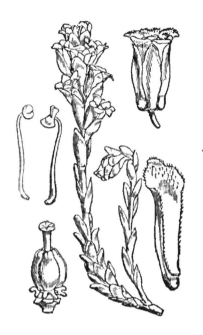

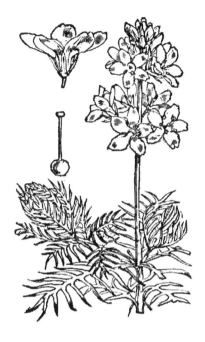

648. Monotropa Hypopithys.

649. Hottonia palustris.

650. Primula vulgaris.

651. Primula veris.

652.   Primula farinosa.

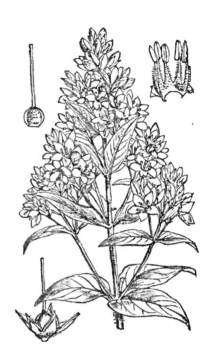

654.   Lysimachia vulgaris.

653.   Cyclamen europæum.

656.   Lysimachia Nummularia.

655.   Lysimachia thyrsiflora.

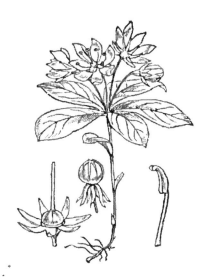

657. Lysimachia nemorum.　　658. Trientalis europæa.

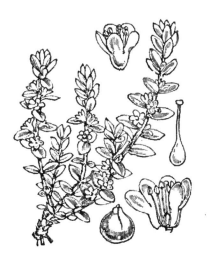

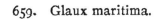

659. Glaux maritima.　　660. Anagallis arvensis.

661.　Anagallis tenella.

662.　Centunculus minimus.

663.　Samolus Valerandi.

664.　Pinguicula vulgaris.

665.　Pinguicula alpina.

666. Pinguicula lusitanica.

667. Utricularia vulgaris.

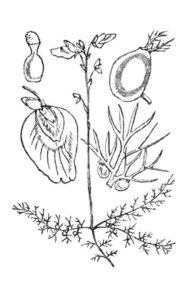

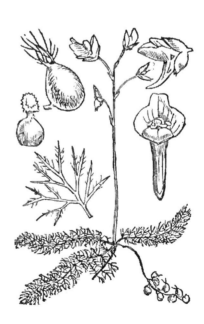

668. Utricularia minor.

669. Utricularia intermedia.

670.   Fraxinus excelsior.   671.   Ligustrum vulgare.

672.   Vinca major.   673.   Vinca minor.

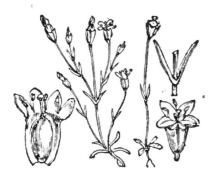

674. Cicendia filiformis.

676. Erythræa Centaurium.

675. Cicendia pusilla.

678. Gentiana verna.

677. Gentiana Pneumonanthe.

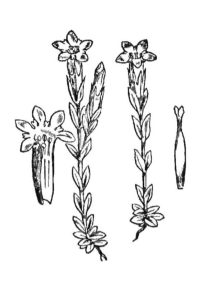

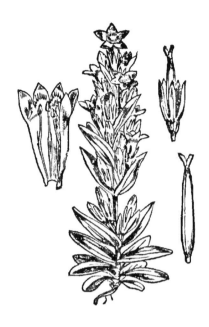

679. Gentiana nivalis.   680. Gentiana Amarella.

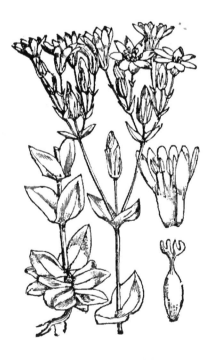

681. Gentiana campestris.   682. Chlora perfoliata.

683. Menyanthes trifoliata.

684. Limnanthemum nym-
phæoides.

685. Polemonium cæruleum.

686. Convolvulus arvensis.

687.　Convolvulus sepium.

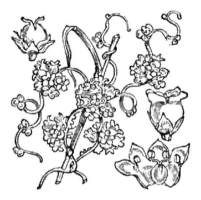

689.　Cuscuta europæa.

690.　Cuscuta Epilinum.

688.　Convolvulus Soldanella.

691.　Cuscuta Epithymum.

692. Echium vulgare.

693. Echium plantagineum.

694. Pulmonaria officinalis.

695. Mertensia maritima.

696. Lithospermum arvense.

697. Lithospermum officinale.

698. Lithospermum purpureo-
cæruleum.

699. Myosotis palustris.

700. Myosotis sylvatica.

701. Myosotis arvensis.

702. Myosotis collina.

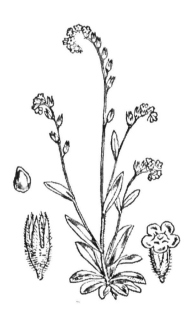

703. Myosotis versicolor.

704.   Anchusa officinalis.

705.   Anchusa sempervirens.

706.   Lycopsis arvensis.

707.   Symphytum officinale.

708. **Symphytum tuberosum.**

709. **Borago officinalis.**

710. **Asperugo procumbens.**

711. **Cynoglossum officinale.**

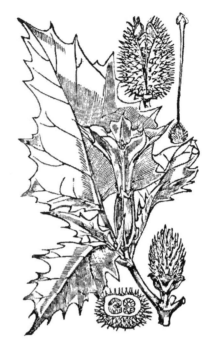

712. Cynoglossum montanum.   713. Datura Stramonium.

714. Hyoscyamus niger.   715. Solanum Dulcamara.

716. Solanum nigrum.

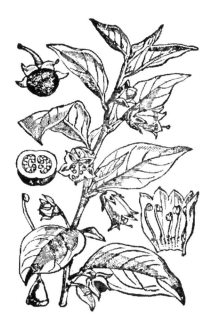

717. Atropa Belladonna.

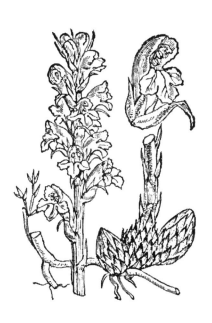

718. Orobanche major.

719. Orobanche caryophyllacea.

720. Orobanche rubra.

721. Orobanche elatior.

722. Orobanche minor.

723. Orobanche cærulea.

724. Orobanche ramosa.

725. Lathræa squamaria.

726. Verbascum Thapsus.

727. Verbascum Blattaria.

728. Verbascum virgatum.

729. Verbascum nigrum.

730. Verbascum Lychnitis.

731. Verbascum pulverulentum.

732. Antirrhinum majus.

733. Antirrhinum Orontium.

734. Linaria vulgaris.

735. Linaria repens.

M

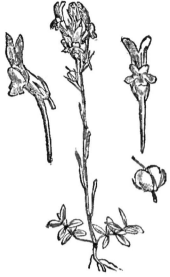

736. Linaria Pelisseriana.

738. Linaria minor.

737. Linaria supina.

739. Linaria Cymbalaria.

740. Linaria spuria.

741. Linaria Elatine.

742. Scrophularia nodosa.

743. Scrophularia aquatica.

744. Scrophularia Scorodonia.

745. Scrophularia vernalis.

746. Mimulus luteus.

747. Limosella aquatica.

748. Sibthorpia europæa.

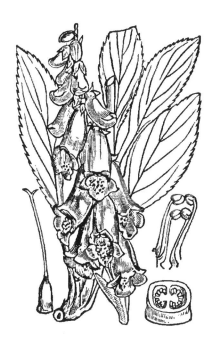

749. Digitalis purpurea.

750. Veronica spicata.

751. Veronica saxatilis.

752. Veronica alpina.

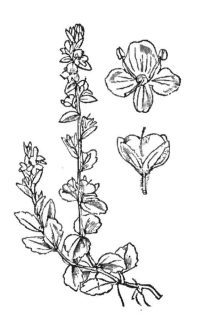

753. Veronica serpyllifolia.

754. Veronica officinalis.

755. Veronica Anagallis.

756. Veronica Beccabunga.

757. Veronica scutellata.

758. Veronica montana.

759. Veronica Chamædrys.

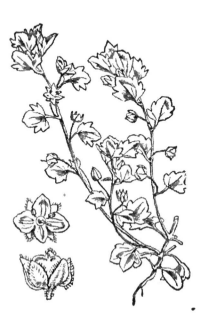

760. Veronica hederæfolia.

761. Veronica agrestis.

762.   Veronica Buxbaumii.   763.   Veronica arvensis.

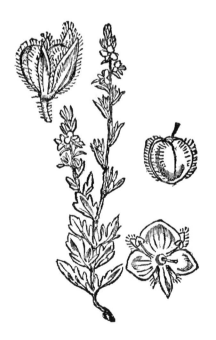

764.   Veronica verna.   765.   Veronica triphyllos.

766. Bartsia alpina.

767. Bartsia viscosa.

768. Bartsia Odontites.

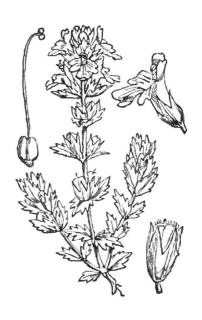

769. Euphrasia officinalis.

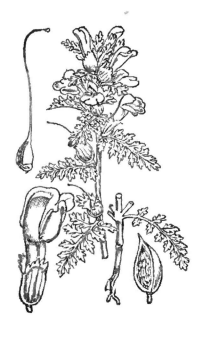

770. Rhinanthus Crista-galli.   771. Pedicularis palustris.

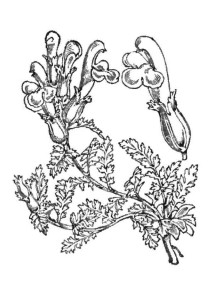

772. Pedicularis sylvatica.   773. Melampyrum cristatum.

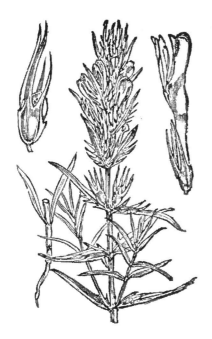

774. Melampyrum arvense.   775. Melampyrum pratense.

776. Melampyrum sylvaticum.   777. Salvia pratensis.

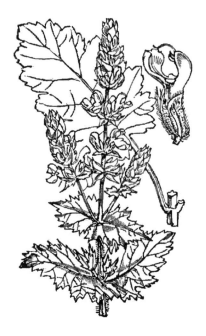

778. Salvia Verbenaca.   779. Lycopus europæus.

780. Mentha sylvestris.   781. Mentha rotundifolia.

782. Mentha viridis.

783. Mentha piperita.

784. Mentha aquatica.

785. Mentha sativa.

786.   Mentha arvensis.

787.   Mentha Pulegium.

788.   Thymus Serpyllum.

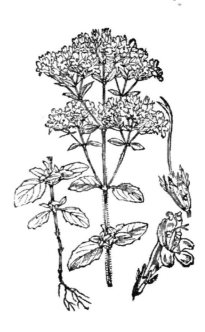

789.   Origanum vulgare.

790. Calamintha Acinos.

791. Calamintha officinalis.

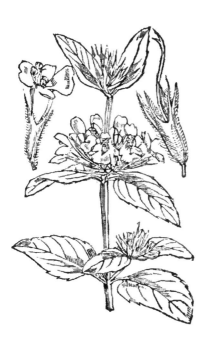

792. Calamintha Clinopodium.

793. Nepeta Glechoma.

794. Nepeta Cataria.

795. Prunella vulgaris.

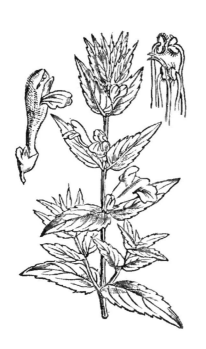

796. Scutellaria galericulata.

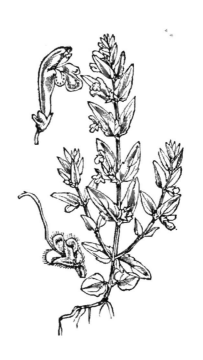

797. Scutellaria minor.

798.   Melittis Melissophyllum.   799.   Marrubium vulgare.

800.   Stachys Betonica.   801.   Stachys germanica.

N

802. Stachys sylvatica.

803. Stachys palustris.

804. Stachys arvensis.

805. Galeopsis Ladanum.

806. Galeopsis ochroleuca.

807. Galeopsis Tetrahit.

808. Ballota nigra.

809. Leonurus Cardiaca.

810.   Lamium amplexicaule.   811.   Lamium purpureum.

812.   Lamium album.   813.   Lamium maculatum.

814. Lamium Galeobdolon.

815. Teucrium Scorodonia.

816. Teucrium Scordium.

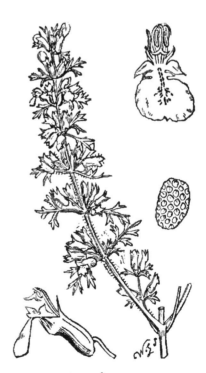

817. Teucrium Botrys.

818. Teucrium Chamædrys.

819. Ajuga reptans.

820. Ajuga genevensis.

821. Ajuga Chamæpitys.

822. Verbena officinalis.

823. Statice Limonium.

824. Statice auriculæfolia.

825. Statice reticulata.

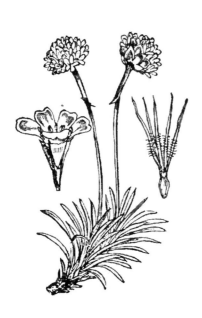

826. Armeria vulgaris.

827. Armeria plantaginea.

828. Plantago major.

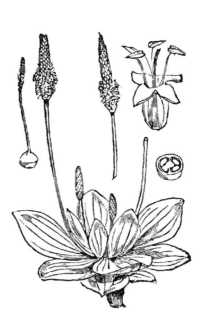

829. Plantago media.

830. Plantago lanceolata.

831. Plantago maritima.

832. Plantago Coronopus.

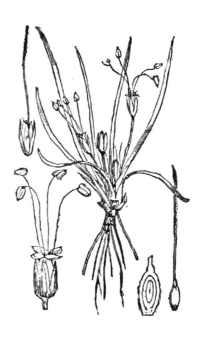

834. Corrigiola littoralis.

833. Littorella lacustris.

835.　Herniaria glabra.

837.　Scleranthus annuus.

836.　Illecebrum verticillatum.

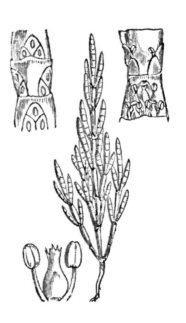

838.　Scleranthus perennis.

839.　Salicornia herbacea.

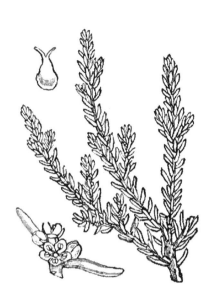

840. Suæda fruticosa.

841. Suæda maritima.

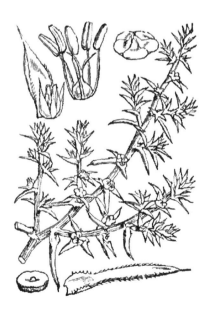

842. Salsola Kali.

843. Chenopodium Vulvaria.

844. Chenopodium polyspermum.

845. Chenopodium album.

846. Chenopodium glaucum.

847. Chenopodium rubrum.

848. Chenopodium urbicum.

849. Chenopodium murale.

850. Chenopodium hybridum.

851. Chenopodium Bonus-
Henricus.

852. Beta maritima.

853. Atriplex portulacoides.

854. Atriplex pedunculata.

855. Atriplex hortensis.

856. Atriplex patula.

857. Atriplex rosea.

858. Rumex aquaticus.

859. Rumex crispus.

860. **Rumex obtusifolius.**

861. **Rumex Hydrolapathum.**

862; **Rumex conglomeratus.**

863. **Rumex sanguineus.**

864. Rumex pulcher.

865. Rumex maritimus.

866. Rumex Acetosa.

867. Rumex Acetosella.

868.   Oxyria reniformis.

869.   Polygonum aviculare.

870.   Polygonum maritimum.

871.   Polygonum Convolvulus.

872. Polygonum dumetorum.

873. Polygonum viviparum.

874. Polygonum Bistorta.

875. Polygonum amphibium.

876.　Polygonum Persicaria.　　　877.　Polygonum lapathifolium.

878.　Polygonum Hydropiper.　　　879.　Polygonum minus.

880. Daphne Mezereum.

881. Daphne Laureola.

882. Hippophae rhamnoides.

883. Thesium linophyllum.

884.   Asarum europæum.   885.   Euphorbia Peplis.

886.   Euphorbia Helioscopia.   887.   Euphorbia platyphyllos.

888.   Euphorbia hiberna.

889.   Euphorbia pilosa.

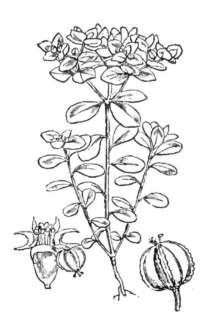

890.   Euphorbia Peplus.

891.   Euphorbia exigua.

892.　Euphorbia Lathyris.

893.　Euphorbia segetalis.

894.　Euphorbia Paralias.

895.　Euphorbia Esula.

896. Euphorbia amygdaloides.

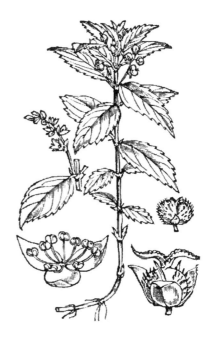

897. Mercurialis perennis.

898. Mercurialis annua.

899. Buxus sempervirens.

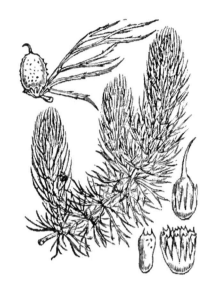

900.   Empetrum nigrum.

901.   Ceratophyllum demersum.

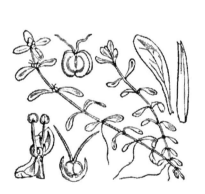

902.   Callitriche aquatica.

903.   Urtica urens.

904. Urtica pilulifera.

905. Urtica dioica.

906. Parietaria officinalis.

907. Humulus Lupulus.

908. **Ulmus montana.**

909. **Ulmus campestris.**

910. **Myrica Gale.**

911. **Alnus glutinosa.**

912. Betula alba.

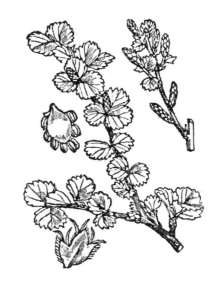

913. Betula nana.

914. Carpinus Betulus.

915. Corylus Avellana.

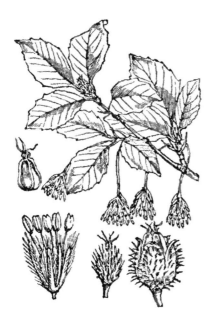

916.   Fagus sylvatica.

917.   Quercus Robur.

918.   Salix pentandra.

919.   Salix fragilis.

920. Salix alba.

921. Salix amygdalina.

922. Salix purpurea.

923. Salix viminalis.

924.　Salix Caprea.

925.　Salix aurita.

926.　Salix phylicifolia.

927.　Salix repens.

928. Salix Lapponum.

930. Salix Myrsinites.

931. Salix reticulata.

929. Salix lanata.

932. Salix herbacea.

933. Populus alba.

934. Populus tremula.

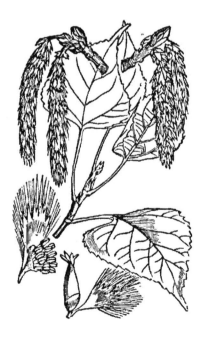

935. Populus nigra.

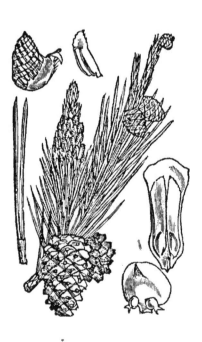

936. Pinus sylvestris.

937. Juniperus communis.

938. Taxus baccata.

939. Typha latifolia.

940. Typha angustifolia.

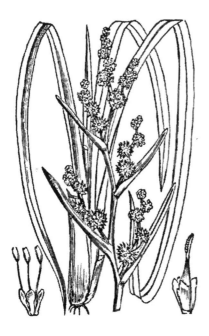

941.　Sparganium ramosum.

942.　Sparganium simplex.

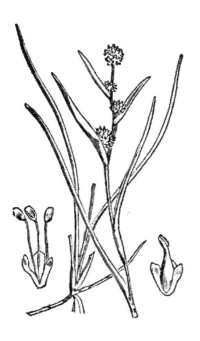

943.　Sparganium minimum.

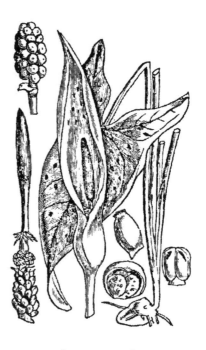

944.　Arum maculatum.

946. Lemna trisulca.

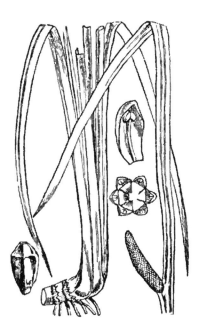

945. Acorus Calamus.

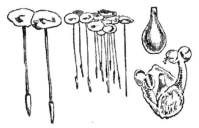

947. Lemna minor.

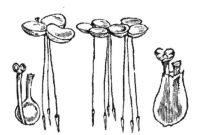

948. Lemna gibba.

949. Lemna polyrrhiza.

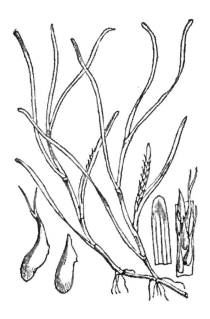

951. Zostera marina.

950. Lemna arrhiza.

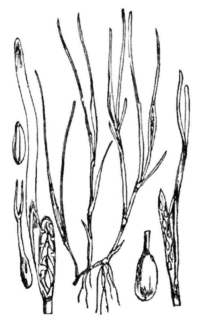

952.   Zostera nana.

953.   Naias flexilis.

954.   Naias marina.

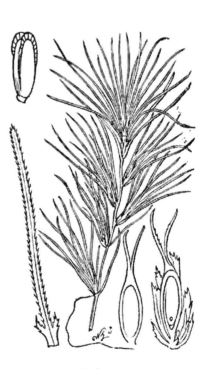

955.   Naias graminea.

956.   Zannichellia palustris.

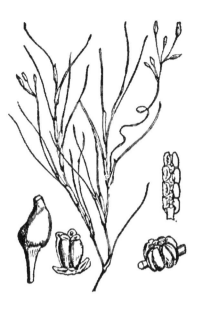

957.   Ruppia maritima.

958.   Potamogeton natans.

959.   Potamogeton heterophyllus

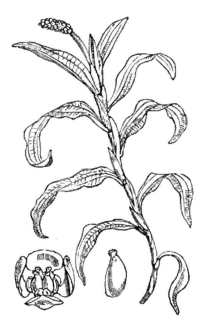

960.   Potamogeton lucens.

961.   Potamogeton prælongus.

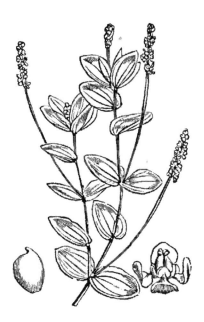

962.   Potamogeton perfoliatus.

963.   Potamogeton crispus.

964. Potamogeton densus.

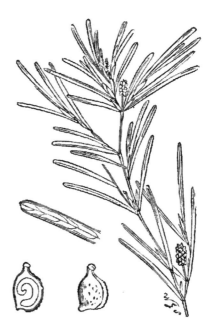

965. Potamogeton obtusifolius.

966. Potamogeton acutifolius.

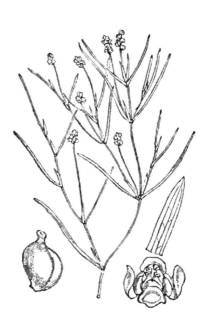

967. Potamogeton pusillus.

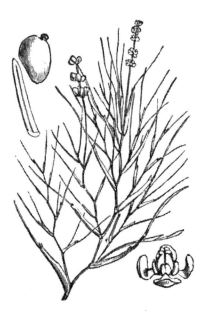

968. Potamogeton pectinatus.

969. Scheuchzeria palustris.

970. Triglochin palustre.

971. Triglochin maritimum.

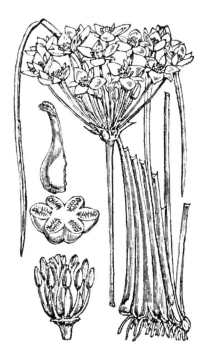

972. Butomus umbellatus.

973. Sagittaria sagittifolia.

974. Alisma Plantago.

975. Alisma ranunculoides.

976.   Alisma natans.

977.   Damasonium stellatum.

¡978.   Elodea canadensis.

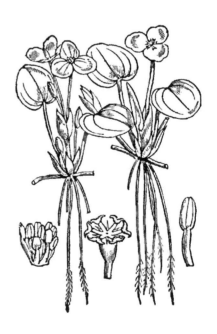

979.   Hydrocharis Morsus-ranæ.

980. Stratiotes aloides.

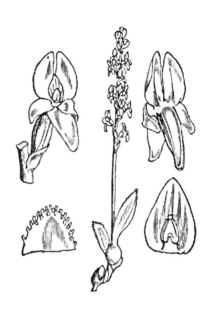

981. Malaxis paludosa.

982. Liparis Loeselii.

983. Corallorhiza innata.

984. Epipactis latifolia.

985. Epipactis palustris.

986. Cephalanthera pallens.

987. Cephalanthera ensifolia.

988. Cephalanthera rubra.

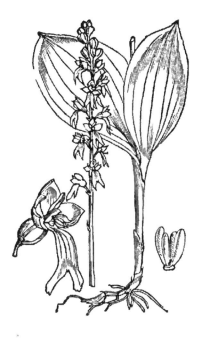

989. Listera ovata.

990. Listera cordata.

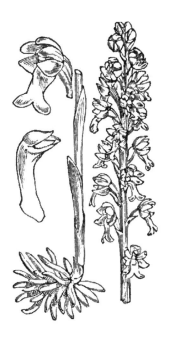

991. Neottia Nidus-avis.

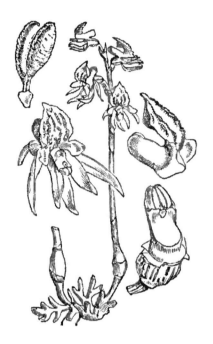

992.   Epipogum aphyllum.

993.   Spiranthes autumnalis.

994.   Spiranthes æstivalis.

995.   Spiranthes Romazoviana.

996.　Goodyera repens.

997.　Orchis Morio.

998.　Orchis militaris.

999.　Orchis ustulata.

1000.   Orchis muscula.

1001.   Orchis laxiflora.

1002.   Orchis maculata.

1003.   Orchis latifolia.

1004. Orchis hircina.

1005. Orchis pyramidalis.

1006. Habenaria bifolia.

1007. Habenaria conopsea.

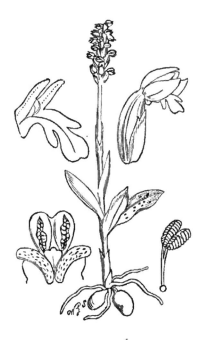

1008. Habenaria intacta.

1009. Habenaria albida.

1010. Habenaria viridis.

1011. Aceras anthropophora.

1012. Herminium Monorchis.

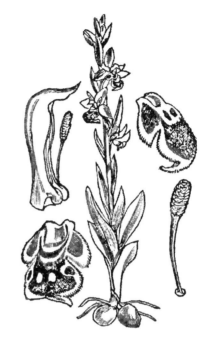

1013. Ophrys apifera.

1014. Ophrys aranifera.

1015. Ophrys muscifera.

1016.   Cypripedium Calceolus.

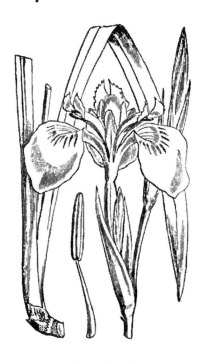

1017.   Iris Pseudacorus.

1018.   Iris fœtidissima.

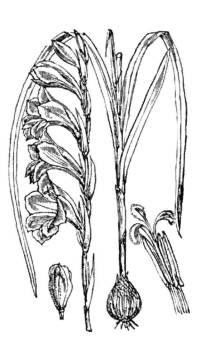

1019.   Gladiolus communis.

1020. Sisyrinchium angustifolium.   1021. Romulea Columnæ.

1022. Crocus vernus.   1023. Crocus nudiflorus.

1024. Narcissus Pseudonarcissus.

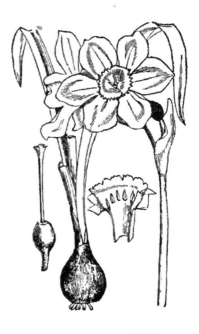

1025. Narcissus biflorus.

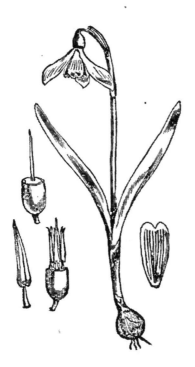

1026. Galanthus nivalis.

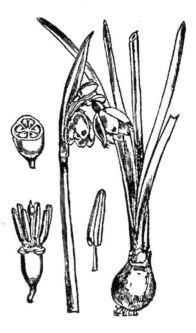

1027. Leucoium æstivum.

1028. Tamus communis.

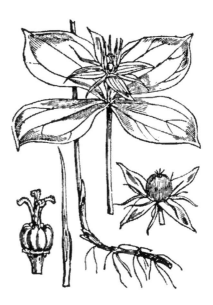

1029. Paris quadrifolia.

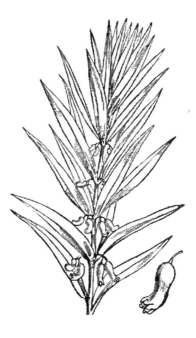

1030. Polygonatum verticillatum.

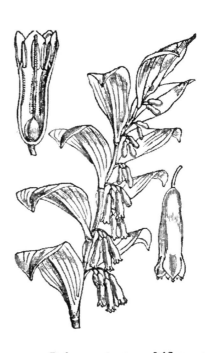

1031. Polygonatum multiflorum.

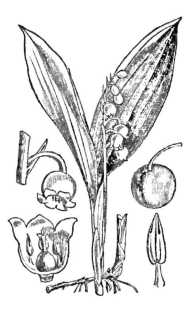

1032. Polygonatum officinale.   1033. Convallaria majalis.

1034. Maianthemum Convallaria.   1035. Asparagus officinalis.

1036. Ruscus aculeatus.

1037. Fritillaria Meleagris.

1038. Tulipa sylvestris.

1039. Lloydia serotina.

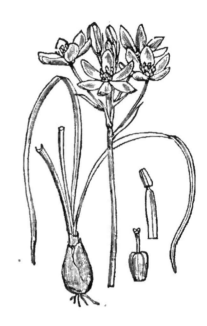

1040. Gagea lutea.

1041. Ornithogalum umbellatum.

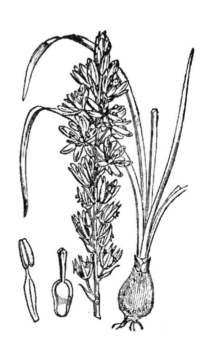

1042. Ornithogalum nutans.

1043. Ornithogalum pyrenaicum.

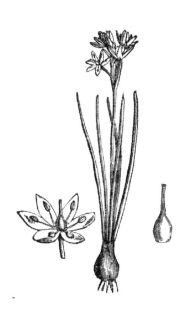

1044. Scilla verna.

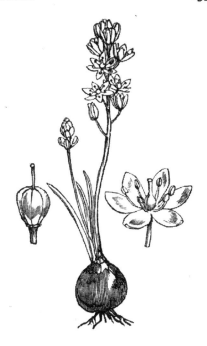

1045. Scilla autumnalis.

1046. Scilla nutans.

1047. Muscari racemosum.

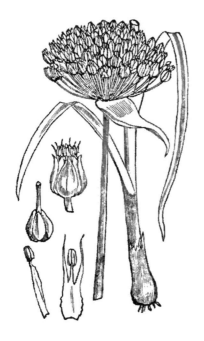

1048. Allium Ampeloprasum.

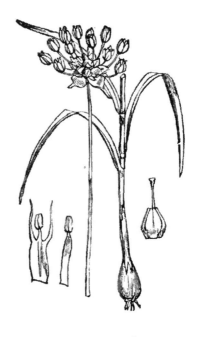

1049. Allium Scorodoprasum.

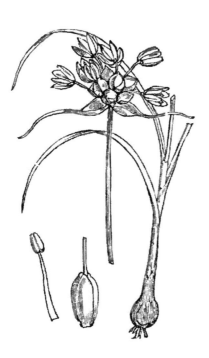

1050. Allium oleraceum.

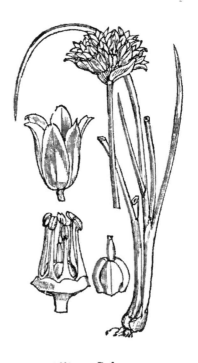

1051. Allium Schœnoprasum.

1052. Allium sphærocephalum.

1053. Allium vineale.

1054. Allium ursinum.

1055. Allium triquetrum.

1056. Simethis bicolor.

1057. Narthecium ossifragum.

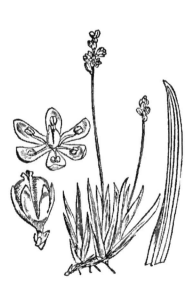

1058. Tofieldia palustris.

1059. Colchicum autumnale.

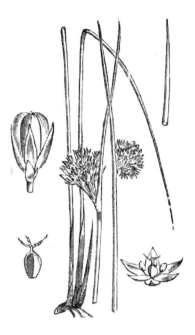

1060. Juncus communis.

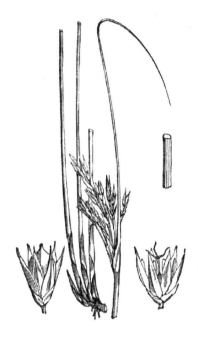

1061. Juncus glaucus.

1062. Juncus filiformis.

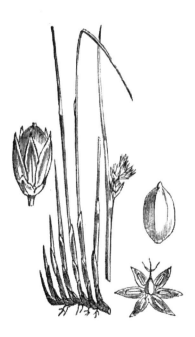

1063. Juncus balticus.

R

1064. Juncus articulatus.

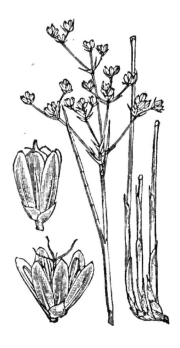

1065. Juncus obtusiflorus.

1066. Juncus compressus.

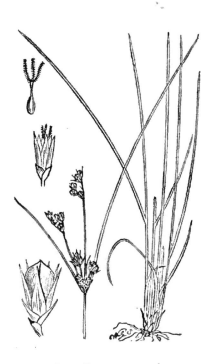

1067. Juncus tenuis.

1068. Juncus squarrosus.

1069. Juncus bufonius.

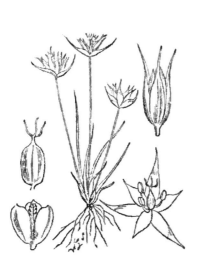

1070. Juncus pygmæus.

1071. Juncus capitatus.

1072. Juncus maritimus.

1073. Juncus acutus.

1074. Juncus trifidus.

1075. Juncus castaneus.

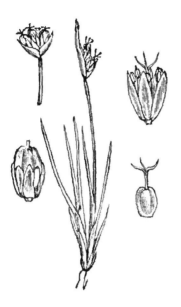

1076. Juncus biglumis.

1077. Luzula pilosa.

1078. Luzula sylvatica.

1079. Luzula arcuata.

1080. Luzula **campestris**.

1081. Luzula spicata.

1082. Eriocaulon septangulare.

1083. Cyperus longus.

1084.   Cyperus fuscus.

1085.   Schœnus nigricans.

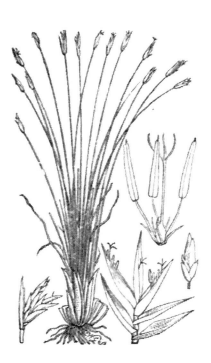

1086.   Schœnus ferrugineus.

1087.   Cladium Mariscus.

1088. Rhynchospora fusca.

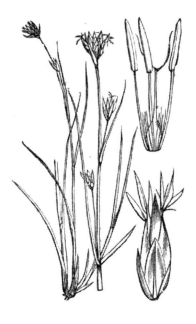

1089. Rhynchospora alba.

1090. Blysmus compressus.

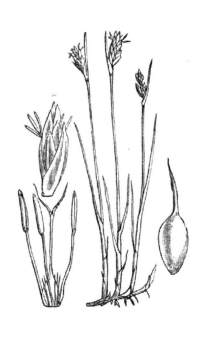

1091. Blysmus rufus.

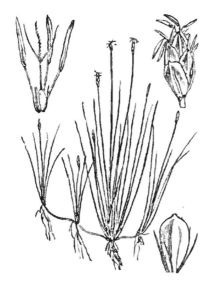

1092. Scirpus acicularis.

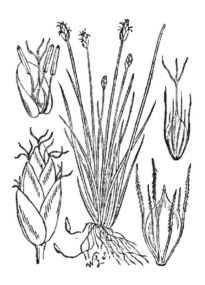

1093. Scirpus parvulus.

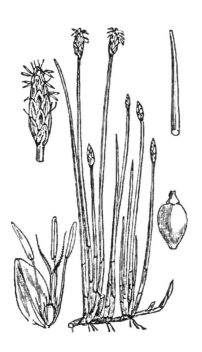

1094. Scirpus palustris.

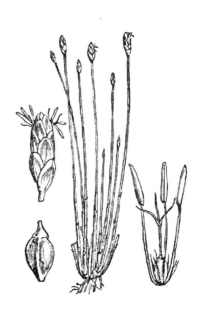

1095. Scirpus multicaulis.

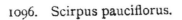

1096. Scirpus pauciflorus.

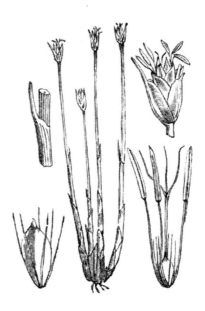

1097. Scirpus cæspitosus.

1098. Scirpus fluitans.

1099. Scirpus setaceus.

1100. Scirpus Savii.

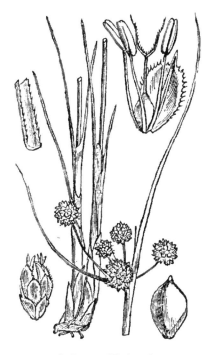

1101. Scirpus Holoschœnus.

1102. Scirpus pungens.

1103. Scirpus triqueter.

1104.   Scirpus lacustris.

1105.   Scirpus maritimus.

1106.   Scirpus sylvaticus.

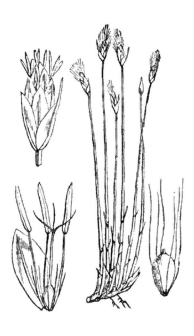

1107.   Eriophorum alpinum.

1108. Eriophorum vaginatum.

1109. Eriophorum polystachion.

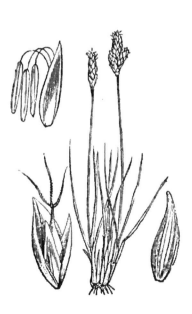

1110. Kobresia caricina.

1111. Carex dioica.

1112. Carex pulicaris.

1113. Carex rupestris.

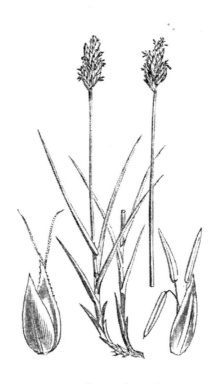

1114. Carex pauciflora.

1115. Carex leporina.

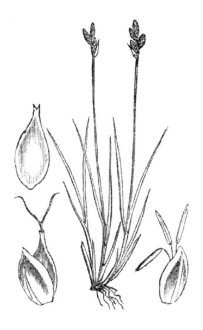

1116. Carex lagopina.

1117. Carex elongata.

1118. Carex echinata.

1119. Carex canescens.

1120.   Carex remota.

1121.   Carex axillaris.

1122.   Carex paniculata.

1123.   Carex vulpina.

1124. Carex muricata.

1125. Carex arenaria.

1126. Carex divisa.

1127. Carex incurva.

1128.   Carex saxatilis.

1129.   Carex cæspitosa.

1130.   Carex acuta.

1131.   Carex alpina.

1132. Carex Buxbaumii.

1133. Carex atrata.

1134. Carex humilis.

1135. Carex digitata.

1136. Carex præcox.

1137. Carex montana.

1138. Carex pilulifera.

1139. Carex tomentosa.

1140. Carex filiformis.

1141. Carex hirta.

1142. Carex pallescens.

1143. Carex extensa.

1144. Carex flava.

1145. Carex distans.

1146. Carex punctata.

1147. Carex panicea.

1148. Carex capillaris.

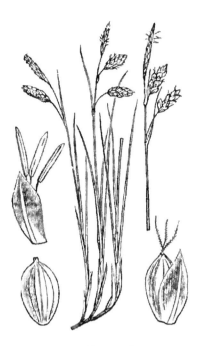

1149. Carex limosa.

1150. Carex glauca.

1151. Carex sylvatica.

1152. Carex strigosa.

1153. Carex Pseudocyperus.

1154. Carex pendula.

1155. Carex ampullacea.

1156.　Carex vesicaria.

1157.　Carex paludosa.

1158.　Leersia oryzoides.

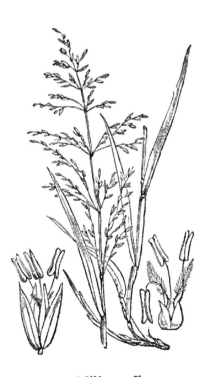

1159.　Milium effusum.

1160. Panicum sanguinale.

1161. Panicum glabrum.

1162. Panicum verticillatum.

1163. Panicum glaucum.

1164. Panicum viride.

1165. Panicum Crus-galli.

1166. Hierochloe borealis.

1167. Anthoxanthum odoratum.

1168.　Phalaris canariensis.

1169.　Digraphis arundinacea.

1170.　Phleum pratense.

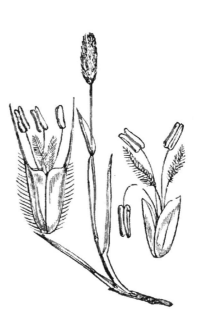

1171.　Phleum alpinum.

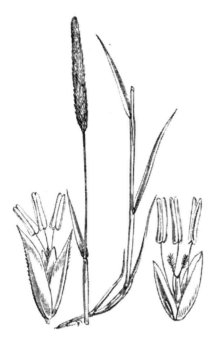

1172. Phleum Bœhmeri.

1173. Phleum asperum.

1174. Phleum arenarium.

1175. Alopecurus agrestis.

1176. Alopecurus pratensis.

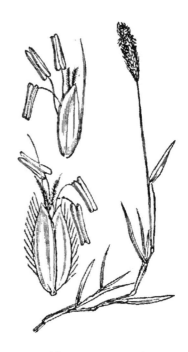

1177. Alopecurus geniculatus.

1178. Alopecurus alpinus.

1179. Mibora verna.

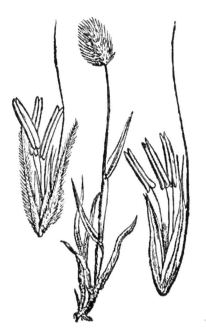

1180.   Lagurus ovatus.

1181.   Polypogon monspeliensis.

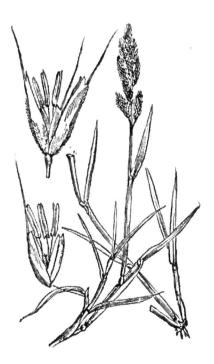

1182.   Polypogon littoralis.

1183.   Agrostis alba.

1184. Agrostis canina.   1185. Agrostis setacea.

1186. Agrostis Spica-venti.   1187. Gastridium lendigerum.

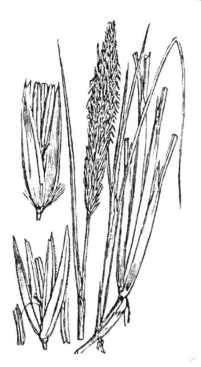

1188. Psamma arenaria.

1189. Calamagrostis Epigeios.

1190. Calamagrostis lanceolata.

1191. Calamagrostis stricta.

T

1192.   Calamagrostis strigosa.

1193.   Aira cæspitosa.

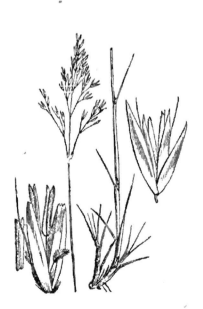

1194.   Aira flexuosa.

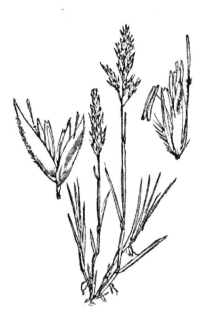

1195.   Aira canescens.

1196.   Aira præcox.

1197.   Aira caryophyllea.

1198.   Avena fatua.

1199.   Avena pratensis.

1200. Avena flavescens.   1201. Arrhenatherum avenaceum.

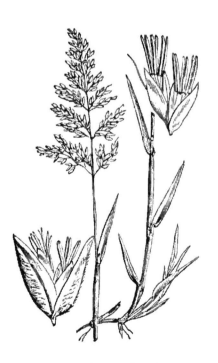

1202. Holcus lanatus.   1203. Holcus mollis.

1204. Cynodon Dactylon.

1206 Lepturus incurvatus.

1205. Spartina stricta.

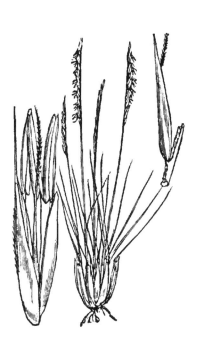

1207. Nardus stricta.

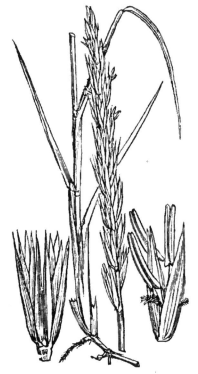

1208. Elymus arenarius.

1210. Hordeum pratense.

1209. Hordeum sylvaticum.

1211. Hordeum murinum.

1212.　Hordeum maritimum.

1214.　Agropyrum caninum.

1213.　Agropyrum repens.

1215.　Lolium perenne.

1216. Lolium temulentum.

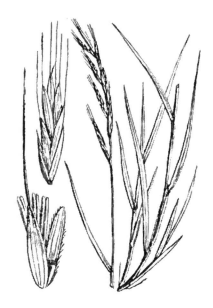

1217. Brachypodium sylvaticum.

1218. Brachypodium pinnatum.

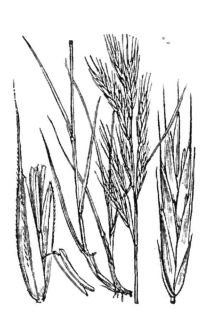

1219. Bromus erectus.

1220.   Bromus asper.

1221.   Bromus sterilis.

1222.   Bromus maximus.

1223.   Bromus madritensis.

1224. Bromus arvensis.

1226. Festuca ovina.

1225. Bromus giganteus.

1227. Festuca elatior.

1228. Festuca sylvatica.

1230. Festuca uniglumis.

1229. Festuca Myuros.

1231. Dactylis glomerata.

1232.   Cynosurus cristatus.   1234.   Briza media.

1233.   Cynosurus echinatus.   1235.   Briza minor.

1236. Poa aquatica.

1238. Poa maritima.

1237. Poa fluitans.

1239. Poa distans.

1240. Poa procumbens.

1241. Poa rigida.

1242. Poa loliacea,

1243. Poa annua.

1244. Poa compressa.

1245. Poa pratensis.

1246. Poa trivialis.

1247. Poa memoralis.

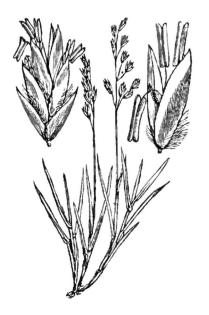

1248.   Poa laxa.

1249.   Poa alpina.

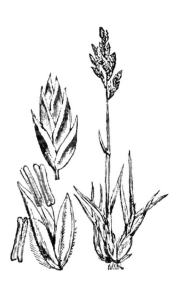

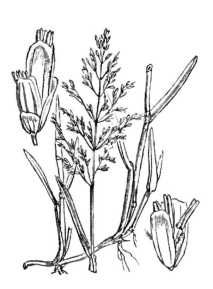

1250.   Poa bulbosa.

1251.   Catabrosa aquatica.

1252.   Molinia cærulea.

1254.   Melica uniflora.

1253.   Melica nutans.

1255.   Triodia decumbens.

U

1256. Kœleria cristata.

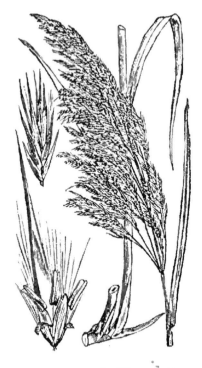

1258. Arundo Phragmites.

1257. Sesleria cærulea.

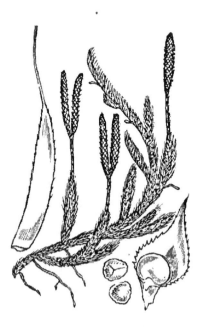

1259. Lycopodium clavatum.

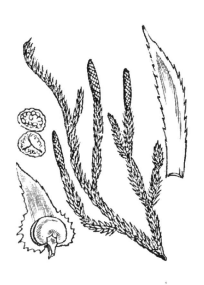

1260. Lycopodium annotinum.

1261. Lycopodium alpinum.

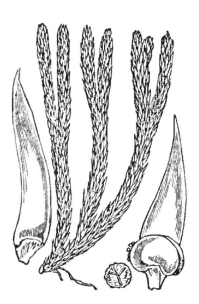

1262. Lycopodium Selago.

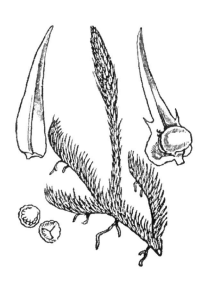

1263. Lycopodium inundatum.

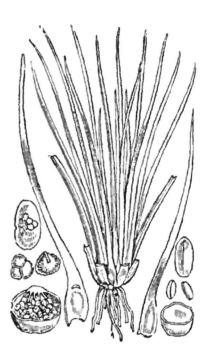

1264. Selaginella selaginoides.   1265. Isoetes lacustris.

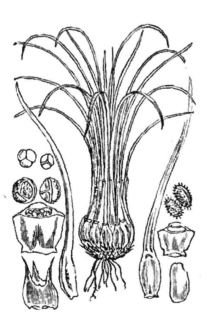

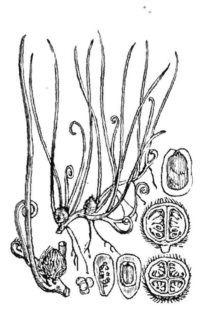

1266. Isoetes Hystrix.   1267. Pilularia globulifera.

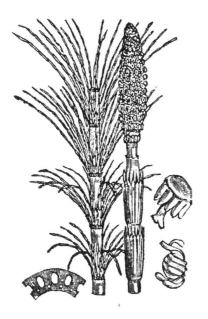

1268. Equisetum Telmateia.

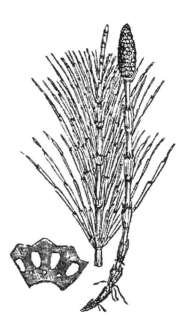

1269. Equisetum arvense.

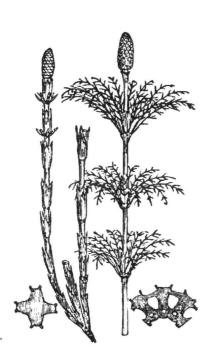

1270. Equisetum sylvaticum.

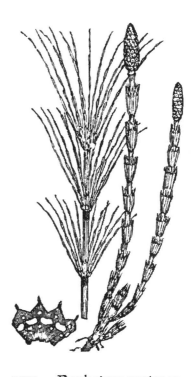

1271. Equisetum pratense.

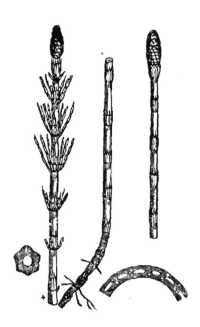

1272.   Equisetum limosum.

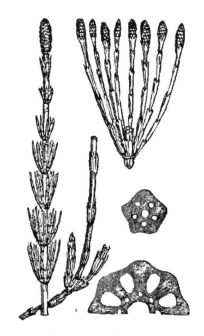

1274.   Equisetum palustre

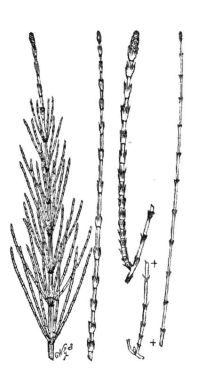

1273.   Equisetum littorale.

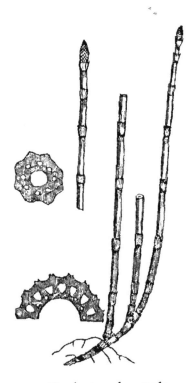

1275.   Equisetum hyemale.

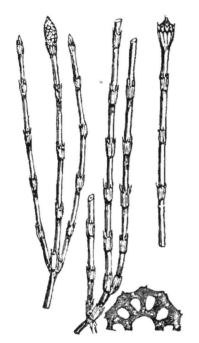

1276.   Equisetum trachyodon.

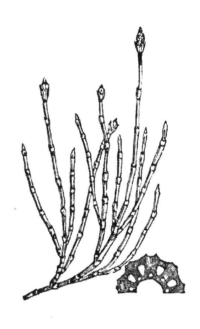

1277.   Equisetum variegatum.

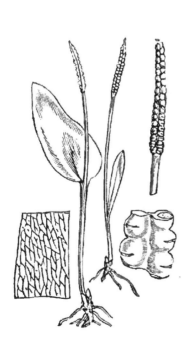

1278.   Ophioglossum vulgatum.

1279.   Botrychium Lunaria.

1280. Osmunda regalis.

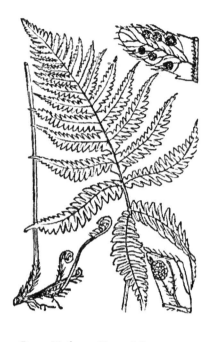

1282. Polypodium Phegopteris.

1281. Polypodium vulgare.

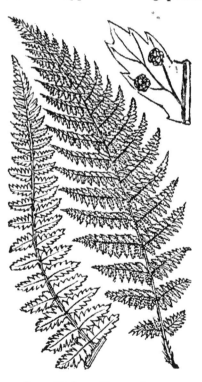

1283. Polypodium alpestre.

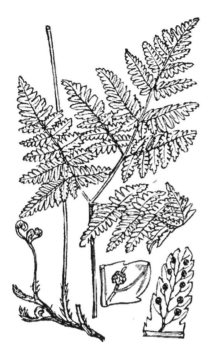

1284.   Polypodium Dryopteris.

1285.   Allosorus crispus.

1286.   Grammitis leptophylla.

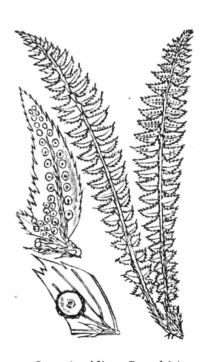

1287.   Aspidium Lonchitis.

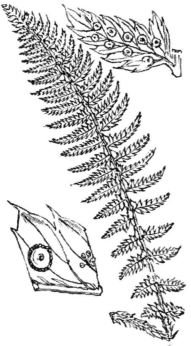

1288. Aspidium aculeatum.

1289. Aspidium Thelypteris.

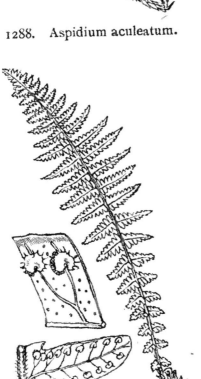

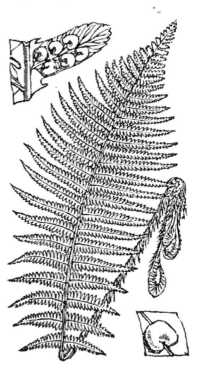

1290. Aspidium Oreopteris.

1291. Aspidium Filix-mas.

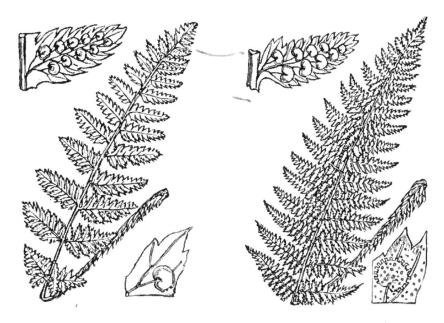

1292. Aspidium cristatum.   1294. Aspidium rigidum.

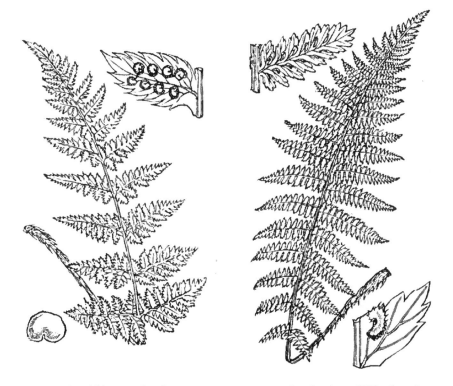

1293. Aspidium spinulosum.   1295. Asplenium Filix-fœmina.

1296.　Asplenium fontanum.

1297.　Asplenium lanceolatum.

1298.　Asplenium marinum.

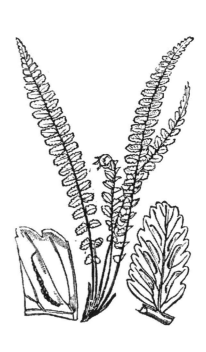

1299.　Asplenium Trichomanes.

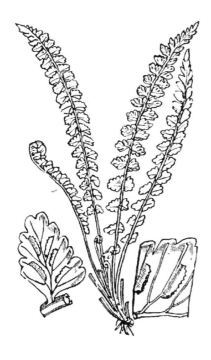

1300. Asplenium viride.

1301. Asplenium Adiantum-
nigrum.

1302. Asplenium Ruta-muraria.

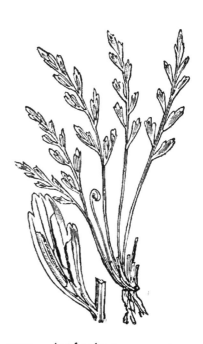

1303. Asplenium germanicum.

1304.　Asplenium septentrionale.

1306.　Ceterach officinarum.

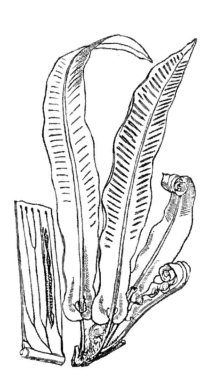

1305.　Scolopendrium vulgare.

1307.　Blechnum Spicant.

1308.   Pteris aquilina.   1309.   Adiantum Capillus-Veneris.

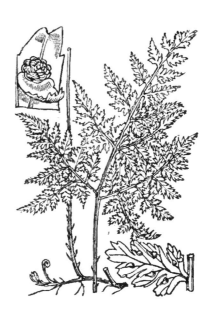

1310.   Cystopteris fragilis.   1311.   Cystopteris montana.

 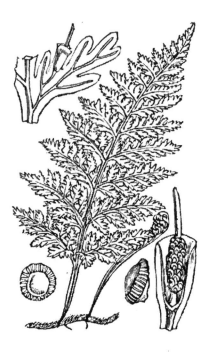

1312. Woodsia ilvensis.   1313. Trichomanes radicans.

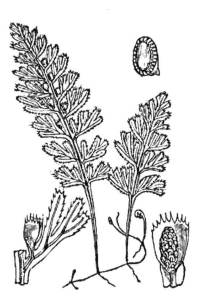 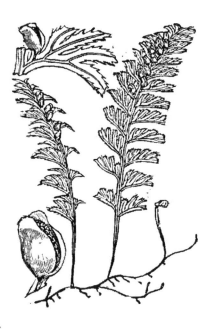

1314. Hymenophyllum   1315. Hymenophyllum
       tunbridgense.   unilaterale.

INDEX.

(Synonyms and names of varieties are in Italics.)

	FIG
ACER campestre	221
Pseudo-platanus	222
Aceras anthropophora	1011
Achillea Millefolium	533
Ptarmica	532
Achyrophorus	
maculatus	587
Aconitum Napellus	30
Acorus Calamus	945
Actæa spicata	31
Actinocarpus	
Damasonium	977
Adiantum	
Capillus-Veneris	1309
Adonis autumnalis	7
Adoxa Moschatellina	461
Ægopodium Podagraria	409
Æthusa cynapium	427
Agraphis nutans	1046
Agrimonia Eupatoria	328
odorata	328
Agropyrum *acutum*	1213
barbata	1213
caninum	1214
junceum	1213
littorale	1213
obtusa	1213
pungens	1213
pycnanthemum	1213
repens	1213
Agrostemma githago	143
Agrostis alba	1183
Anemagrostis	1186
canina	1184
interrupta	1186
nigra	1183
pumila	1183
setacea	1185
Spica-venti	1186
stolonifera	1183
sub-repens	1183
vulgaris	1183
Aira *alpina*	1193
cæspitosa	1193
canescens	1195
caryophyllea	1197
discolor	1193
flexuosa	1194
lævigata	1193
montana	1194
præcox	1196

	FIG.
setacea	1194
uliginosa	1194
Ajuga Chamæpitys	821
genevensis	820
pyramidalis	820
reptans	819
Alchemilla alpina	324
argentea	324
arvensis	325
conjuncta	324
hybrida	323
montana	323
phanes	325
vulgaris	323
Alisma *lanceolatum*	974
natans	976
Plantago	974
ranunculoides	975
repens	975
Alliaria officinalis	73
Allium	
Ampeloprasum	1048
arenarium	1049
Babingtonii	1048
bulbiferum	1049
carinatum	1050
compactum	1053
complanatum	1050
Halleri	1049
holmense	1049
oleraceum	1050
Porrum	1048
Schœnoprasum	1051
Scorodoprasum	1049
Sibiricum	1051
sphærocephalum	1052
triquetrum	1055
ursinum	1054
vineale	1053
Allosorus crispus	1285
Alnus glutinosa	911
Alopecurus agrestis	1175
alpinus	1178
bulbosus	1177
fulvus	1177
geniculatus	1177
palustris	1177
pratensis	1176
pronus	1177
Watsoni	1178
Alsine Cherleri	150

	FIG.
stricta	152
tenuifolia	153
verna	151
Althæa hirsuta	200
officinalis	199
Alyssum calycinum	87
maritimum	88
Ammophila	
arundinacea	1188
baltica	1188
Anacamptis	
pyramidalis	1005
Anacharis *Alsinastrum*	978
canadensis	978
Anagallis arvensis	660
cœrulea	660
phœnicea	660
tenella	661
Anchusa *arvensis*	706
officinalis	704
sempervirens	705
Andromeda polifolia	633
Anemone nemorosa	6
Pulsatilla	5
Angelica sylvestris	434
Antennaria dioica	512
hyperborea	512
margaritacea	513
Anthemis *anglica*	529
arvensis	529
Cotula	528
maritima	529
nobilis	530
tinctoria	531
Anthoxanthum	
odoratum	1167
Puelii	1167
Anthriscus sylvestris	445
vulgaris	446
Anthyllis *Dillenii*	268
Vulneraria	268
Antirrhinum majus	732
Orontium	733
Apargia autumnalis	583
hispida	582
Taraxaci	583
Apera interrupta	1186
Spica-venti	1186
Apium graveolens	404
inundatum	406
nodiflorum	405

X

	FIG.
ochneatum . . .	405
Aporanthus Trifoli-	
astrum . . .	244
Aquilegia vulgaris .	28
Arabis alpina . .	59
ciliata . . .	60
glabrata . . .	58
hirsuta . . .	58
hispida . . .	62
perfoliata . .	56
petræa . . .	63
sagittata . . .	58
stricta . . .	62
Thaliana . .	61
Turrita . . .	57
Arbutus Unedo .	630
Arctium intermedium	555
Lappa . . .	555
majus . . .	555
minus . . .	555
nemorosum . .	555
pubens . . .	555
sub-tomentosum .	555
tomentosum . .	555
Arctostaphylos alpina	632
Uva-ursi . .	631
Arenaria Cherleri .	150
ciliata . . .	156
Gerardi . . .	151
glutinosa . .	155
gottaica . .	156
hirta . . .	151
hybrida . .	153
laxa . . .	153
leptoclados . .	155
marginata . .	171
norvegica . .	156
peploides . .	154
rubella . . .	151
rubra . . .	171
serpyllifolia .	155
sphærocarpa .	155
sulcata . . .	151
tenuifolia . .	153
trinervis . .	157
uliginosa . .	152
verna . . .	151
viscosa . . .	153
Armeria duriuscula .	826
maritima . .	826
planifolia . .	826
plantaginea . .	827
pubescens . .	826
pubigera . .	826
scotica . .	826
vulgaris . .	826
Armoracia amphibium	55
rusticana . .	85
Arnoseris pusilla .	610
Arrhenatherum aven-	
aceum . . .	1201
bulbosa . .	1201
elatius . .	1201
Artemisia Absinthium	539
campestris . .	536
gallica . . .	537
maritima . .	537
vulgaris . .	538

	FIG.
Arthrolobium ebrac-	
teatum . .	274
Arum italicum . .	944
maculatum . .	944
Arundo Calamagrostis	1190
Phragmites .	1258
Asarum europæum .	884
Asparagus officinalis	1035
Asperugo procumbens	710
Asperula cynanchica	482
odorata . .	481
Aspidium aculeatum .	1288
æmulum . .	1293
angulare . .	1288
Bootii . .	1293
cristatum . .	1292
dilatatum . .	1293
dumetorum . .	1293
Filix-mas . .	1291
lobatum . .	1288
lonchitidoides .	1288
Lonchitis . .	1287
Oreopteris . .	1290
remotum . .	1293
rigidum . .	1294
spinulosum . .	1293
Thelypteris .	1289
Asplenium acutum .	1301
Adiantum-nigrum .	1301
alternifolium .	1303
anceps . .	1299
Ceterach . .	1306
Clermontæ .	1299
convexa . .	1295
Filix-fœmin .	1295
fontanum . .	1296
germanicum .	1303
incisum . .	1295
lanceolatum .	1297
marinum . .	1298
molle . . .	1295
obtusum . .	1301
Petrarchæ .	1299
rhæticum . .	1295
Ruta-muraria .	1302
septentrionale .	1304
serpentini . .	1301
Trichomanes .	1299
viride . .	1300
Aster Linosyris .	499
Tripolium . .	498
Astragalus alpinus .	270
danicus . .	269
glycyphyllos .	271
hypoglottis .	269
Astrantia major .	400
Athyrium alpestre .	1283
Filix fœmina .	1295
latefolium . .	1295
Atriplex angustifolia .	856
arenaria . .	857
Babingtonii .	856
deltoidea . .	856
erecta . .	856
farinosa . .	857
hastata . .	856
hortensis . .	855
laciniata . .	857

	FIG.
litoralis . . .	856
marina . . .	856
nitens . . .	855
patula . . .	856
pedunculata . .	854
portulacoides .	853
prostrata . .	856
rosea . . .	857
serrata . . .	856
Smithii . . .	856
triangularis . .	856
Atropa belladonna .	717
Avena alpina . .	1199
elatior . .	1201
fatua . .	1198
flavescens . .	1200
planiculmis . .	1199
pratensis . .	1199
pubescens . .	1199
strigosa . .	1198
Azalia procumbens .	634
BALLOTA alba . .	808
fœtida . .	808
nigra . . .	808
ruderalis . .	808
Barbarea arcuata .	51
intermedia .	51
parviflora . .	51
præcox . .	51
stricta . .	51
vulgaris . .	51
Barkhausia fœtida .	597
taraxacifolia .	596
Bartsia alpina . .	766
divergens . .	768
Odontites . .	768
serotina . .	768
verna . .	768
viscosa . .	767
Bellis perennis .	504
Berberis vulgaris .	33
Beta maritima . .	852
Betonica officinalis	800
Betula alba . .	912
glutinosa . .	912
nana . . .	913
pendula . .	912
verrucosa . .	912
Bidens cernua .	521
tripartita . .	522
Blackstonia perfoliata	682
Blechnum boreale .	1307
Spicant . .	1307
Blysmus compressus	1090
rufus . . .	1091
Borago officinalis	709
Botrychium Lunaria	1279
rutaceum . .	1279
Brachypodium	
pinnatum . .	1213
sylvaticum .	1217
Brassica adpressa .	84
alba . . .	81
Babingtonii .	77
brevipes . .	77
Briggsii . .	80
campestris . .	80

	FIG.
Cheiranthus . .	78
monensis . .	78
muralis . .	77
napus . .	80
nigra . .	83
oleifera . .	80
oleracea . .	79
polymorpha . .	80
Rapa . .	80
rapifera . .	80
Ruta-baga . .	80
sativa . .	80
Sinapis . .	82
Sinapistrum . .	82
sylvestris . .	80
tenuifolia . .	76
Briza media . .	1234
minor . .	1235
Bromus arvensis .	1224
asper . .	1220
Benekenii . .	1220
commutatus . .	1224
curtisii . .	1223
diandrus . .	1223
erectus . .	1219
giganteus . .	1225
glabrescens . .	1224
hordeaceus . .	1224
Lloydianus . .	1224
madritensis . .	1223
maximus . .	1222
molliformis . .	1224
mollis . .	1224
multiflorus . .	1224
pratensis . .	1224
racemosus . .	1224
ramosus . .	1220
rigidus . .	1223
secalinus . .	1224
serotinus . .	1220
sterilis . .	1221
velutinus . .	1224
villosa . .	1219
Brunella vulgaris .	795
Bryonia dioica .	358
Bulbocastanum Linnæi	414
Bunium	
bulbocastanum . .	414
flexuosum . .	443
Bupleurum aristatum	420
falcatum . .	422
Odontites . .	420
rotundifolium . .	419
tenuissimum . .	421
Butomus umbellatus .	972
Buxus sempervirens .	809
CAKILE	
americana . .	111
maritima . .	111
Calamagrostis	
Epigejos . .	1189
lanceolata . .	1190
lapponica . .	1191
stricta . .	1191
strigosa . .	1192
Calamintha Acinos .	790
arvensis . .	790

	FIG.
Briggsii . .	791
Clinopodium . .	792
Nepeta . .	791
officinalis . .	791
sylvatica . .	791
Callitriche aquatica .	902
autumnalis . .	902
hamulata . .	902
Lachii . .	902
obtusangula . .	902
pedunculata . .	902
platycarpa . .	902
stagnalis . .	902
truncata . .	902
verna . .	902
vernalis . .	902
Calluna	
erica . .	642
vulgaris . .	642
Caltha	
Guerangetii minos .	24
palustris . .	24
radicans . .	24
riparia . .	24
vulgaris . .	24
Calystegia Sepium	687
Soldanella . .	688
Camelina *fœtida* . .	94
sativa . .	94
Campanula glomerata .	617
hederacea . .	624
hybrida . .	625
lancifolia . .	623
latifolia . .	619
montana . .	623
patula . .	622
persicifola . .	622
Rapunculoides . .	620
Rapunculus . .	621
rotundifolia . .	623
Trachelium . .	618
Capsella Bursa-pastoris	102
Cardamine amara .	64
bulbifera . .	68
dentata . .	65
flexuosa . .	67
hastulata . .	63
Heyneana . .	65
hirsuta . .	67
impatiens . .	66
pratensis . .	65
sylvatica . .	67
Carduus acanthoides .	560
acaulis . .	569
arvensis . .	564
crispus . .	560
eriophorus . .	565
Forsteri . .	563
heterophyllus . .	566
lanceolatus . .	562
Marianus . .	558
nutans . .	559
palustris . .	563
polyanthemus . .	560
pratensis . .	568
pycnocephalus . .	561
setosus . .	564
tenuiflorus . .	561

	FIG.
tuberosus . .	567
Woodwardsii . .	568
Carex acuta . .	1130
alpicola . .	1119
alpigena . .	1136
alpina . .	1131
ampullacea . .	1155
aquatilis . .	1129
arenaria . .	1125
argyrolochin . .	1115
atrata . .	1133
axillaris . .	1121
binervis . .	1145
Bœnninghauseniana	1121
Buxbaumii . .	1132
cæspitosa . .	1129
canescens . .	1119
capillaris . .	1148
ciliata . .	1135
clandestina . .	1134
collina . .	1137
curta . .	1119
Davalliana . .	1111
depauperata . .	1145
dichroa . .	1126
digitata . .	1135
dioica . .	1111
distans . .	1145
disticha . .	1125
divisa . .	1126
divulsa . .	1124
ebracteata . .	1141
echinata . .	1118
Ehrhartiana . .	1122
elongata . .	1117
ericetorum . .	1135
extensa . .	1143
filiformis . .	1140
flava . .	1144
frigida . .	1147
fulva . .	1145
Gibsoni . .	1129
glauca . .	1150
Goodenovii . .	1129
gracilis . .	1130
Grahami . .	1128
Grypos . .	1118
hirta . .	1141
hirtæformis . .	1141
Hornschuchiana .	1145
humilis . .	1134
incurva . .	1127
intermedia . .	1125
involuta . .	1156
irrigua . .	1149
lævigata . .	1145
lagopina . .	1116
Leesii . .	1138
lepidocarpa . .	1144
leporina . .	1115
ligerica . .	1125
limosa . .	1149
Micheliana . .	1150
mielichoferi . .	1147
montana . .	1137
muricata . .	1124
Œderi . .	1144
ornithopoda . .	1135

	FIG.
ovalis	1115
pallescens	1142
paludosa	1157
panicea	1147
paniculata	1122
paradoxa	1122
pauciflora	1114
pendula	1154
Persoonii	1119
phæostachya	1147
pilulifera	1138
polygama	1132
præcox	1136
Pseudocyperus	1153
Pseudo-divulsa	1124
Pseudo-paradoxa	1122
pulicaris	1112
pulla	1128
punctata	1146
rariflora	1149
recurva	1150
remota	1120
rigida	1129
riparia	1157
rostrata	1155
rupestris	1113
salina	1147
saxatilis	1128
Saxumbra	1138
scotica	1147
spadicea	1157
sparsiflora	1147
speirostachya	1145
spicata	1124
stellulata	1118
stictocarpa	1150
stricta	1129
strigosa	1152
sylvatica	1151
tenella	1120
teretiuscula	1122
tomentosa	1139
tricostata	1130
trinervis	1129
vaginata	1147
Vahlii	1131
vesicaria	1136
vitilis	1119
vulgaris	1129
vulpina	1123
Watsoni	1129
Xanthocarpa	1145
Carlina vulgaris	571
Carpinus Betulus	914
Carum Bulbocastanum	414
Carvi	413
flexuosum	443
Petroselinum	410
segetum	411
verticillatum	412
Catabrosa aquatica	1251
litoralis	1251
minor	1251
Caucalis Anthriscus	448
arvensis	449
dancoides	450
helvetica	449
infesta	449

	FIG.
latifolia	451
nodosa	447
Centaurea aspera	575
Calcitrapa	576
Cyanus	574
decipiens	572
Isnardi	575
nigra	572
nigrescens	572
Scabiosa	573
solstitialis	577
Centranthus ruber	484
Centunculus minimus	662
Cephalanthera ensifolia	987
grandiflora	986
pallens	986
rubra	988
Cerastium *alpestre*	160
alpinum	162
Andrewsii	161
aquaticum	164
arvense	161
atrovirens	160
Edmondstonii	162
glomeratum	160
glutinosum	160
holosteoides	160
lanatum	162
latifolium	162
nigrescens	162
pentandrum	160
pubescens	161
pumilum	160
quaternellum	158
semidecandrum	160
Smithii	162
tetrandrum	160
trigynum	163
triviale	160
viscosum	160
vulgatum	160
Ceratophyllum	
apiculatum	901
demersum	901
submersum	901
Ceterach officinarum	1306
Chærophyllum	
Anthriscus	446
sativum	445
sylvestre	445
temulentum	444
temulum	444
Chamagrostis minima	1179
Cheiranthus cheiri	50
Chelidonium	
laciniatum	42
majus	42
Chenopodina maritima	841
Chenopodium	
acutifolium	844
album	845
Bonus-henricus	851
botryodes	847
candicans	845
deltoideum	848
ficifolium	845
glaucum	846
hybridum	850

	FIG.
intermedium	848
murale	849
olidum	843
paganum	845
polyspermum	844
pseudo-botryodes	847
rubrum	847
urbicum	848
virens	845
viride	845
Vulvaria	843
Cherleria sedoides	150
Chlora perfoliata	682
Chrysanthemum	
inodorum	526
Leucanthemum	523
Parthenium	525
segetum	524
Chrysocoma Linosyris	499
Chrysosplenium	
alternifolium	390
oppositifolium	389
Cicendia filiformis	674
pusilla	675
Cichorium Intybus	609
Cicuta virosa	403
Cineraria integrifolia	552
Circæa alpina	354
intermedia	354
lutetiana	353
Cistus anglicus	118
marifolius	118
tomentosus	119
Cladium *germanicum*	1087
Mariscus	1087
Claytonia *alsinoides*	174
perfoliata	174
Clematis Vitalba	1
Clinopodium vulgare	792
Cnicus acaulis	569
arvensis	564
Carolorum	566
dubius	569
eriophorus	565
Forsteri	568
heterophyllus	566
horridus	564
lanceolatus	562
palustris	563
pratensis	568
setosus	564
tuberosus	567
Woodwardsii	568
Cochlearia *alpina*	86
anglica	86
Armoracia	85
danica	86
greenlandica	86
Hortii	86
littoralis	86
officinalis	86
polymorpha	86
Colchicum autumnale	1059
Comarum palustre	322
Conium maculatum	453
Conopodium	
denudatum	443
Convallaria majalis	1033

	FIG.
Convolvulus arvensis	686
sepium	687
Soldanella	688
Conyza squarrosa	517
Corallorhiza innata	983
Coriandrum sativum	456
Cornus sanguinea	460
suecica	459
Coronopus didyma	109
Ruellii	108
Corrigiola littoralis	834
Corydalis *bulbosa*	47
claviculata	47
lutea	46
solida	47
Corylus Avellana	915
Corynephorus	
canescens	1195
Cotoneaster vulgaris	340
Cotyledon *foliosa*	360
Umbilicus	360
Crambe maritima	112
Cratægus *monogyna*	339
Oxyacantha	339
Oxyacanthoides	339
Crepis biennis	599
fœtida	597
hieracioides	600
paludosa	601
setosa	596
succisæfolia	600
taraxacifolia	596
tectorum	598
virens	598
Crithmum maritimum	433
Crocus nudiflorus	1023
speciosus	1023
vernus	1022
Cryptogramme crispa	1285
Cucubalus Behen	135
Cuscuta Epilinum	690
Epithymum	691
europæa	689
Trifolii	691
Cyclamen europæum	653
hederæfolium	653
neapolitanum	653
Cynodon Dactylon	1204
Cynoglossum	
montanum	712
officinale	711
sylvaticum	712
Cynosurus cristatus	1232
echinatus	1233
Cyperus fuscus	1084
longus	1083
Cypripedium	
Calceolus	1016
Cystopteris *alpina*	1310
dentata	1310
Dickieana	1310
fragilis	1310
montana	1311
Cytisus *prostrata*	232
scoparius	232
Dabeocia polifolia	635
Dactylis glomerata	1231

	FIG.
Damasonium stellatum	977
Danthonia decumbens	1255
Daphne Laureola	881
Mezereum	880
Datura Stramonium	712
Daucus Carota	452
gummifer	452
maritimus	452
Delphinium Ajacis	29
Consolida	29
Demazeria loliacea	1227
Dentaria *bulbifera*	68
Deschampsia cæspitosa	1193
flexuosa	1194
Deyeuxia Hookeri	1191
neglecta	1191
Dianthus Armeria	130
cæsius	132
Caryophyllus	132
deltoides	131
glaucus	131
plumarius	132
prolifer	129
Digitalis purpurea	749
Digitaria filiformis	1161
humifusa	1161
sanguinalis	1160
Digraphis arundinacea	1169
Diotis maritima	534
Diplotaxis Babingtonii	77
muralis	77
tenuifolia	76
Dipsacus *Fullonum*	492
pilosus	493
sylvestris	492
Doronicum	
Pardalianches	553
plantagineum	554
Draba aizoides	89
confusa	91
contorta	91
hirta	90
incana	91
muralis	92
rupestris	90
verna	93
Drosera anglica	394
intermedia	393
longifolia	393
rotundifolia	392
Dryas *depressa*	304
octopetala	304
Echinochloa Crus-galli	1165
Echium *italicum*	692
Plantagineum	693
violaceum	693
vulgare	692
Elatine hexandra	177
Hydropiper	178
tripetala	177
Eleocharis acicularis	1092
cæspitosa	1097
multicaulis	1095
palustris	1094
parvula	1093
pauciflora	1096
uniglumis	1094

	FIG.
Watsoni	1094
Eleogiton fluitans	1098
Elisma natans	976
Elodea canadensis	978
Elymus arenarius	1208
europæus	1209
geniculatus	1208
Empetrum nigrum	900
Endymion nutans	1046
Enodium cæruleum	1252
Epilobium alpinum	350
alsinefolium	349
anagallidifolium	350
angustifolium	342
brachycarpum	342
hirsutum	343
intermedium	344
Lamyi	347
lanceolatum	345
montanum	345
obscurum	347
palustre	348
parviflorum	344
rivulare	344
roseum	346
tetragonum	347
virgatum	347
Epipactis *atrorubens*	984
Helleborine	984
latifolia	984
media	984
ovalis	984
palustris	985
purpurata	984
rubiginosa	984
varians	984
violacea	984
viridiflora	984
Epipogum aphyllum	992
Gmelini	992
Equisetum *alpina*	1274
arenarium	1277
arvense	1269
Drummondii	1271
fluviatile	1268
hyemale	1275
limosum	1272
littorale	1273
Mackaii	1276
maximum	1265
Moorei	1275
paleaceum	1275
palustre	1274
polystachia	1274
pratense	1271
ramosum	1276
subnuda	1274
sylvaticum	1270
Telmatela	1268
trachyodon	1276
umbrosum	1271
variegatum	1277
Wilsoni	1277
Erica carnea	640
ciliaris	639
cinerea	637
hibernica	640
Mackaiana	638

		FIG.
Mackayi	. .	638
mediterranea	.	640
Tetralix	.	638
vagans	. .	641
Watsoni	.	639
Erigeron acre	.	500
alpinum	.	501
canadense	.	502
uniflorus	.	501
Eriocaulon		
septangulare	.	1082
Eriophorum alpinum		1107
angustifolium	.	1109
gracile	. .	1109
latifolium	.	1109
polystachion	.	1109
pubescens	. .	1109
vaginatum	.	1108
Erodium *chærophyllum*	214
cicutarium	.	214
commixtum	.	214
hirtum	.	214
maritimum	.	216
moschatum	.	215
pimpinellæfolium	214
Erophila brachycarpa	93
inflata	. .	93
vulgaris	. .	93
Erucastrum incana	84
Eryngium campestre	.	402
maritimum	.	401
Erysimum *Alliaria*	.	73
cheiranthoides	.	74
orientale	. .	75
Erythræa *capitata*	.	676
Centaurium	.	676
chloodes	.	676
conferta	. .	676
latifolia . .	676
linarifolia	.	676
littoralis	.	676
pulchella	. .	676
Eupatorium		
cannabinum	.	497
Euphorbia		
amygdaloides	.	896
Cyparissias	.	895
Esula	. .	895
exigua	. .	891
Helioscopia	.	886
hiberna	. .	888
Lathyris	. .	892
palustris	. .	889
Paralias	. .	894
Peplis	. .	885
Peplus	. .	890
pilosa	. .	889
platyphyllos	.	887
portlandica	.	893
segetalis	.	893
stricta	. .	887
Euphrasia *gracilis*	.	769
maritima	. .	769
nemorosa	. .	769
Odontites	. .	768
officinalis	.	769
rotundata	.	768
viscosa	. .	767

		FIG.
Evonymus europæus	.	224
Exacum filiforme	.	674
FAGUS sylvatica	.	916
Falcatula		
ornithopodioides	244
Fedia Auricula	.	490
carinata	. .	489
dentata	. .	491
olitoria	. .	488
Festuca *ambigua*	.	1229
arenaria	. .	1226
arundinacea		1227
bromoides .	.	1229
cæsia	. .	1226
calamaria	.	1228
decidua	.	1228
duriuscula	.	1226
elatior	.	1227
gigantea	. .	1225
glauca	. .	1226
loliacea	. .	1227
major	.	1226
Myuros	.	1229
oraria	. .	1226
ovina	.	1226
pratensis	.	1227
procumbens	.	1240
Pseudo-myuros	.	1229
rigida	. .	1241
rubra	.	1226
sabulicola	.	1226
sciuroides .	.	1229
sylvatica	.	1228
tenuifolia .	.	1226
triflora	. .	1225
uniglumis	.	1230
vivipara	. .	1226
Fibichia umbellata	.	1204
Filago *apiculata* .	.	505
canescens	.	505
gallica	.	507
germanica	.	505
Jussiæi	.	505
lutescens	.	505
minima	.	506
montana	.	506
spathulata	.	505
Fœniculum *officinale*	.	428
vulgare	.	428
Fragaria *elatior*	.	312
sterilis	.	313
vesca	.	312
Frankenia lævis	.	128
Fraxinus excelsior	.	670
heterophylla	.	670
Fritillaria Meleagris	1037
Fumaria *agraria*	.	45
Boræi	. .	45
capreolata	.	45
confusa	.	45
densiflora .	.	45
media	. .	45
micrantha	.	45
muralis	.	45
officinalis	.	45
pallidiflora	.	45
parviflora .	.	45

		FIG
tenuisecta .	. .	45
Vaillantii	. .	45
GAGEA *fascicularis*	.	1010
lutea .	. .	1040
Galanthus nivalis	.	1026
Galeobdolon luteum	814
Galeopsis *angustifolia*	805
bifida	. .	807
canescens .	.	805
dubia	. .	806
intermedia	. .	805
Ladanum .	.	805
ochroleuca	.	806
speciosa	. .	807
Tetrahit	.	807
versicolor .	.	807
Galium anglicum		477
Aparine	.	479
aristatum	.	476
Bakeri	. .	476
boreale	.	478
commutatum	.	475
Cruciata .	.	471
elatum	. .	476
elongatum	.	473
erectum	. .	476
insubricum	.	476
Mollugo .	.	476
montanum	.	475
nitidulum	.	475
ochroleucum	.	472
palustre	.	473
pusillum .	.	475
saxatile	.	475
scabrum	.	476
spurium	.	479
sylvestre .	.	475
tricorne	.	480
uliginosum	.	474
Vaillantii	.	479
verum	.	472
Witheringii	.	473
Gastridium		
lendigerum		1187
Genista anglica	.	231
humifusa	.	229
pilosa	.	230
prostrata	.	229
tinctoria	.	229
Gentiana Amarella	.	680
campestris	.	681
germanica	.	680
nivalis	.	679
Pneumonanthe		677
præcox	. .	680
uliginosa .	.	680
verna	.	678
Geranium		
carolinianum		212
columbinum	.	213
dissectum	.	212
lancastriense	.	202
Lebelii	.	207
lucidum	.	208
modestum	.	207
molle	.	209
perenne	.	206

	FIG
phœum	203
pratense	205
prostratum	202
purpureum	207
pusillum	210
pyrenaicum	206
Rau	208
Robertianum	207
rotundifolium	211
sanguineum	202
sylvaticum	204
Geum *intermedium*	306
rivale	306
urbanum	305
Githago segetum	143
Gladiolus communis	1019
illyricus	1019
Glaucium luteum	44
violaceum	43
Glaux maritima	659
Glechoma hederacea	793
Glyce maritima	88
Glyceria aquatica	1236
Borreri	1239
conferta	1239
declinata	1237
distans	1239
fluitans	1237
hispida	1238
loliacea	1242
maritima	1238
pedicellata	1237
plicata	1237
procumbens	1240
rigida	1241
spectabilis	1236
Gnaphalium	
luteo-album	508
norvegicum	509
pilulare	511
rectum	509
supinum	510
sylvaticum	509
uliginosum	511
Goodyera repens	996
Grammitis leptophylla	1286
Gymnadenia albida	1009
conopsea	1007
Gymnogramma lepto-phylla	1286
HABENARIA albida	1009
bifolia	1006
chlorantha	1006
conopsea	1007
intacta	1008
viridis	1010
Haloscias scoticum	430
Hedera *canariensis*	457
Helix	457
Hedypnois hirtus	584
hispidus	582
Taraxaci	583
Helianthemum	
Breweri	117
canum	118
guttatum	117
marifolium	118

	FIG
polifolium	120
surrejanum	119
vineale	118
vulgare	119
Heliocharis, see *Eleocharis*.	
Helleborus fœtidus	27
viridis	26
Helminthia echioides	580
Helosciadium	
inundatum	406
nodiflorum	405
ochreatum	405
repens	405
Heracleum	
angustifolium	439
Sphondylium	439
Herminium Monorchis	1012
Herniaria *ciliata*	835
glabra	835
hirsuta	835
Hesperis matronalis	69
Hieracium *acutifolium*	610
aggregatum	604
alpinum	603
amplexicaulis	605
anglicum	605
argenteum	604
atratum	603
aurantiacum	602
boreale	607
Borreri	608
cæsium	604
calenduliflorum	603
canadense	606
cenereum	604
cerinthoides	605
chrysanthum	603
cinerascens	604
corymbosum	608
crocatum	608
decipiens	605
denticulatum	608
Dewari	604
divaricatum	603
eximium	603
filifolium	606
flocculosum	604
Gibsoni	604
globosum	603
gothicum	604
gracilentum	603
heterophyllum	607
holosericeum	603
hypochœroides	604
inuloides	608
Iricum	605
juranum	608
Lapeyrousii	605
lasiophyllum	604
latifolium	604
Lawsoni	603
lingulatum	603
macrocephalum	604
maculatum	604
melanocephalum	603
microcephalum	603
molle	600

	FIG
murorum	604
nemorosum	604
nigrescens	603
nitidum	604
obtusifolium	604
pallidum	604
paludosum	601
Peletierianum	602
Pilosella	602
pilosissimum	602
prenanthoides	608
pulmonarium	603
rigidum	608
rubescens	604
sabaudum	607
saxifragum	603
senescens	603
stelligerum	604
sylvaticum	604
tenellum	603
tridentatum	604
umbellatum	606
villosum	603
vulgatum	604
Hierochloe borealis	1166
Hippocrepis comosa	276
Hippophae	
rhamnoides	882
Hippuris vulgaris	397
Holcus lanatus	1202
mollis	1203
Holosteum umbellatum	159
Honckenya peploides	154
Hordeum maritimum	1212
murinum	1211
pratense	1210
sylvaticum	1209
Hottonia palustris	649
Humulus Lupulus	907
Hutchinsia petræa	101
Hyacinthus nonscriptus	1046
Hydrocharis	
Morsus-ranæ	979
Hydrocotyle vulgaris	398
Hymenophyllum	
alatum	1313
tunbridgense	1314
unilaterale	1315
Wilsoni	1315
Hyoscyamus niger	714
Hypericum	
Androsæmum	180
anglicum	180
angustifolium	181
bœticum	183
calycinum	179
decumbens	185
dubium	182
Elodes	189
hirsutum	187
humifusum	184
linarifolium	185
maculatum	183
montanum	188
perforatum	181
pulchrum	186
quadrangulum	183
quadratum	183

	FIG
tetrapterum	183
undulatum	183
Hypochœris *Balbisii*	585
glabra	585
maculata	587
radicata	586
Hypopithys multiflora	648
IBERIS amara	100
Ilex Aquifolium	223
Illecebrum	
verticillatum	836
Impatiens *biflora*	220
fulva	220
Noli-me-tangere	219
parviflora	219
Inula Conyza	517
crithmoides	516
dysenterica	518
Helenium	514
Pulicaria	519
salicina	515
Iris *acoriformis*	1017
Bastardi	1017
fœtidissima	1018
Pseudacorus	1017
Isatis tinctoria	110
Isnardia palustris	352
Isoetes *Duriœi*	1265
echinospora	1265
hystrix	1266
lacustris	1265
Morei	1265
Isolepis fluitans	1098
Holoschœnus	1101
pygmœa	1100
Saviana	1100
Savii	1100
setacea	1099
JASIONE montana	614
Juncus *acutiflorus*	1064
acutus	1073
arcticus	1063
articulatus	1064
balticus	1063
biglumis	1076
bottnicus	1066
bufonius	1069
bulbosus	1066
capitatus	1071
castaneus	1075
cœnosus	1066
communis	1060
compressus	1066
conglomeratus	1060
diffusus	1061
effusus	1060
filiformis	1062
Gerardi	1066
glaucus	1061
lamprocarpus	1064
maritimus	1072
nigritellus	1064
obtusiflorus	10€5
pygmæus	1070
squarrosus	1068
subverticillatus	1064

	FIG
supinus	1064
sylvaticus	1064
tenuis	1067
trifidus	1074
triglumis	1076
uliginosus	1064
Juniperus communis	937
nana	937
Knappia agrostidea	1179
Knautia arvensis	496
Kobresia caricina	1110
Kœleria cristata	1256
Kœniga maritima	88
LACTUCA alpina	591
muralis	588
saligna	590
Scariola	589
virosa	589
Lagurus ovatus	1180
Lamium album	812
amplexicaule	810
dissectum	811
Galeobdolon	814
hybridum	811
incisum	811
intermedium	810
laevigatum	813
maculatum	813
purpureum	811
Lapsana communis	611
Lastrea abbreviata	1291
œmula	1294
collina	1293
cristata	1292
dilatata	1293
Filix-mas	1291
Oreopteris	1290
recurva	1294
remota	1293
rigida	1294
spinulosa	1293
Thelypteris	1289
uliginosa	1292
Lathræa squamaria	725
Lathyrus	
acutifolius	295
Aphaca	289
hirsutus	290
latifolius	293
macrorrhizus	296
maritimus	295
niger	297
Nissolia	288
palustris	294
pratensis	291
sylvestris	293
tuberosus	292
Lavatera arborea	195
Olbia	195
Leersia oryzoides	1158
Lemna arrhiza	950
gibba	948
Michelii	950
minor	947
polyrrhiza	949
trisulca	946

	FIG
Leontodon autumnalis	583
hastilis	582
hirtus	584
hispidus	582
pratensis	583
Taraxacum	595
Leonurus Cardiaca	809
Lepidium *alatostyla*	103
campestre	103
Draba	105
hirtum	103
latifolium	106
ruderale	107
Smithii	104
Lepigonum medium	171
neglectum	171
rubrum	171
rupestre	171
rupicola	171
salinum	171
Lepturus *filiformis*	1206
incurvatus	1206
Leucojum æstivum	1027
vernum	1027
Libanotis montana	429
Ligusticum scoticum	430
Ligustrum vulgare	671
Limnanthemum	
nymphæoides	684
peltatum	684
Limosella aquatica	747
Linaria Cymbalaria	739
Elatine	741
latifolia	734
minor	738
Pelisseriana	736
repens	735
sepium	735
speciosa	734
spuria	740
striata	735
supina	737
vulgaris	734
Linnæa borealis	469
Linosyris vulgaris	499
Linum angustifolium	192
catharticum	193
perenne	191
usitatissimum	190
Liparis Loeselii	982
Listera cordata	990
ovata	989
Lithospermum arvense	696
officinale	697
purpureo-cærulenm	698
Littorella lacustris	833
Lloydia serotina	1039
Lobelia Dortmanna	612
urens	613
Lobularia maritima	88
Loiseleuria procumbens	634
Lolium	
aristata	1215
arvense	1216
festucaceum	1215
italicum	1215
multiflorum	1215
perenne	1215

	FIG.
remotum . . .	1215
temulentum . .	1216
Lomaria Spicant .	1307
Lonicera	
Caprifolium . .	467
Periclymenum . .	466
Xylosteum . .	468
Loroglossum hircinium	1004
Lotus angustissimus .	267
corniculatus .	266
crassifolius .	266
decumbens .	266
deflexus . .	267
diffusus . .	267
hispidus . .	267
major . .	266
pilosus . .	266
tenuifolius .	266
tenuis . .	266
uliginosus .	266
villosus . .	266
Ludwigia palustris .	352
Luzula arcuata . .	1079
Borreri . .	1077
campestris .	1080
congesta . .	1080
erecta . .	1080
Forsteri . .	1077
maxima . .	1078
multiflora .	1080
pilosa . .	1077
spicata . .	1081
sylvatica . .	1078
vernalis . .	1077
Lychnis *alba* . .	141
alpina . .	146
dioica . .	142
diurna . .	142
Flos-cuculi .	144
Githago . .	143
vespertina .	141
Viscaria . .	145
Lycopodium alpinum .	1261
annotinum .	1260
clavatum . .	1259
complanatum .	1261
inundatum .	1263
selaginoides .	1264
Selago . .	1262
Lycopsis arvensis .	706
Lycopus europæus .	779
Lynosiris vulgaris .	499
Lysimachia nemorum	657
Nummularia .	656
punctata . .	654
thyrsiflora .	655
vulgaris . .	654
Lythrum hyssopifolium	356
Salicaria . .	355
MAIANTHEMUM	
bifolium . .	1034
Convalaria .	1034
Malachium aquaticum	164
Malaxis paludosa .	981
Malva *borealis* .	196
moschata . .	198
parviflora . .	196

	FIG
pusila . . .	196
rotundifolia . .	196
sylvestris . .	197
verticillata . .	196
Marrubium vulgare .	799
Matricaria Chamomilla	527
inodora . .	526
maritima . .	526
Parthenium . .	525
salina . .	526
Matthiola incana .	48
sinuata . .	49
Meconopsis cambrica .	41
Medicago *apiculata* .	238
arabica . .	239
denticulata .	238
falcata . .	235
lappacea . .	238
lupulina . .	237
maculata . .	239
minima . .	240
sativa . .	236
sylvestris . .	235
Melachium aquaticum	164
Melampyrum arvense	774
cristatum . .	773
latifolia . .	775
montanum . .	775
pallidiflora .	776
pratense . .	775
sylvaticum .	776
Melica nutans . .	1253
uniflora . .	1254
Melilotus alba . .	243
altissima . .	241
arvensis . .	242
leucantha . .	243
officinalis . .	241
vulgaris . .	243
Melittis *grandiflora* .	798
Melissophyllum .	798
Mentha *agrestis* . .	786
Allioni . .	786
alopecuroides .	780
aquatica . .	784
arvensis . .	786
cardiaca . .	785
citrata . .	784
crispa . .	782
erecta . .	787
gentilis . .	785
gracilis . .	785
hircina . .	784
hirsuta . .	784
mollissima .	780
nemorosa . .	780
nummularia .	786
officinalis . .	783
paludosa . .	785
palustris . .	784
parietariæfolia .	786
Pauliana . .	785
piperita . .	783
præcox . .	786
pratensis . .	785
pubescens . .	784
Pulegium . .	787
rivalis . .	785

	FIG
rotundifolia . .	781
rubra . .	785
sativa . .	785
subglabra . .	784
sylvestris .	730
velutina . .	785
viridis . .	782
vulgaris . .	783
Wirtgeniana .	785
Menyanthes trifoliata	683
Menziesia cærulea .	636
polifolia . .	635
Mercurialis *ambigua* .	898
annua . .	898
perennis . .	897
Mertensia maritima .	695
Mespilus germanica .	341
Meum athamanticum .	432
Mibora verna . .	1179
Microcala filiformis .	674
Milium effusum . .	1159
Mimulus luteus . .	746
Mœhringia trinervia .	157
Mœnchia erecta . .	158
Molinia cærulea . .	1252
depauperata .	1252
Moneses grandiflora	643
Monotropa Hypopi-	
tys . .	648
Montia fontana . .	175
minor . .	175
rivularis . .	175
Mulgedium alpinum	591
Muscari racemosum .	1047
Myosotis *alpestris* .	700
arvensis . .	701
cæspitosa . .	699
collina . .	702
intermedia . .	701
lingulata . .	699
Mitteni . .	702
palustris . .	699
repens . .	699
rupicola . .	700
strigulosa . .	699
sylvatica . .	700
umbrosa . .	701
versicolor . .	703
Myosurus minimus .	8
Myrica Gale . .	910
Myriophyllum	
alterniflorum .	395
pectinatum .	396
spicatum . .	395
verticillatum .	396
Myrrhis odorata . .	442
NAIAS flexilis . .	953
graminea . .	955
major . .	954
marina . .	954
Narcissus biflorus .	1025
Bromfieldii .	1024
cambricus . .	1024
lobularis . .	1024
major . .	1024
Pseudonarcissus .	1024
Nardus stricta . .	1207

	FIG.
Narthecium	
ossifragum . . 1057	
Nasturtium amphibium	55
microphyllum . . 52	
officinale . . 52	
palustre . . 54	
siifolium . . 52	
sylvestre . . 53	
terrestre . . 54	
Neotinia intacta . 1008	
Neottia Nidus-avis . 991	
Nepeta Cataria . 794	
Glechoma . 793	
Nephrodium abbreviata 1291	
œmulum . . 1293	
affinis . . 1291	
Borreri . . 1291	
cristatum . . 1292	
dilatatum. . 1293	
Filix-mas. . 1291	
fœnisecii . . 1293	
glandulosa . 1293	
incisa . . 1291	
montanum . 1290	
nana. . . 1293	
Oreopteris. . 1290	
rigidum . . 1294	
spinulosum . 1293	
Thelypteris . 1289	
Nuphar *intermedium*. 35	
luteum . . 35	
minimum. . 35	
pumilum . . 35	
Nymphœa alba . 34	
Odontites divergens . 768	
rotundata. . 768	
rubra . . 768	
serotina . . 768	
verna . . 768	
Œnanthe crocata . 425	
fistulosa . . 423	
fluviatilis . . 426	
Lachenalii . 424	
peucedanifolia. 424	
Phellandrium . 426	
pimpinelloides . 424	
silaifolia . . 424	
Smithii . . 424	
Œnothera biennis . 351	
odorata . . 351	
Onobrychis sativa . 277	
viciæfolia . . 277	
Ononis *antiquorum* . 233	
arvensis . . 233	
campestris . 233	
horrida . . 233	
inermis . . 233	
maritima . . 233	
procumbens . 233	
procurrens . 233	
reclinata . . 234	
repens . . 233	
spinosa . . 233	
Onopordon Acanthium 570	
Ophioglossum	
ambigua . . 1278	
lusitanicum . 1278	

	FIG.
vulgatum . . 1278	
Ophrys apifera . 1013	
arachnites . 1013	
aranifera . 1014	
fucifera . 1014	
muscifera . . 1015	
Trollii . 1013	
Orchis *angustifolia* . 1003	
fusca . . 998	
hircina . . 1004	
incarnata. . 1003	
latifolia . 1003	
laxiflora . 1001	
maculata . . 1002	
majalis . 1003	
mascula . 1000	
militaris . 998	
Morio . 997	
palmata . . 1003	
purpurea . 998	
pyramidalis . 1005	
Simia . 998	
tephrosanthos . 998	
ustulata . . 999	
Origanum	
megastachyum . 789	
vulgare . . 789	
Ornithogalum *luteum*. 1040	
nutans . . 1042	
pyrenaicum . 1043	
umbellatum . 1041	
Ornithopus ebracteatus 274	
perpusillus . 275	
Orobanche *amethystea* 722	
arenaria . . 723	
barbata . . 722	
cærulea . . 723	
caryophyllacea 719	
elatior . . 721	
Epithymum . 720	
Eryngii . . 722	
Galii . . 719	
Hederæ . . 722	
major . . 718	
minor . . 722	
Picridis . . 722	
ramosa . . 724	
Rapum . . 718	
rubra . . 720	
Orobus macrorrhizus . 206	
niger . . 297	
sylvaticus. . 282	
tenuifolius . 296	
tuberosus . . 296	
Osmunda regalis . 1280	
Oxalis Acetosella . 217	
corniculata . 218	
stricta . . 218	
Oxycoccus palustris . 629	
Oxyria *digyna* . 868	
reniformis . 868	
Oxytropis campestris . 272	
Halleri . . 273	
uralensis . . 273	
PÆONIA *corallina* . 32	
officinalis . . 32	
Panicum Crus-galli . 1165	

	FIG.
glabrum . . 1161	
glaucum . . 1163	
sanguinale . 1160	
verticillatum . 1162	
viride . . 1164	
Papaver Argemone . 40	
dubium . . 33	
hybridum . . 39	
Lamottei . . 38	
Lecoqii . . 38	
Rhœas . . 37	
somniferum . 36	
strigosum . . 37	
Parietaria *diffusa* . 906	
officinalis . 906	
Paris quadrifolia . 1029	
Parnassia palustris . 391	
Pastinaca sativa . 438	
Pedicularis palustris . 771	
sylvatica . 772	
Peplis Portula . 357	
Petasites vulgaris . 541	
Petroselinum sativum 410	
Segetum . . 411	
Peucedanum officinale 435	
Ostruthium . 437	
palustre . . 436	
sativum . . 438	
Phaca astragalina . 269	
Phalaris *arundinacea*. 1169	
canariensis . 1168	
Phegopteris Dryopteris 1284	
polypodioides . 1282	
Phellandrium	
aquaticum . . 426	
Phleum alpinum . 1171	
arenarium . 1174	
asperum . 1173	
Bœhmeri . 1172	
nodosum . . 1170	
phalaroides . 1172	
pratense . 1170	
stolonifera . 1170	
Phragmites communis 1258	
Phyllodoce cœrulea . 636	
taxifolia . . 636	
Physospermum	
cornubiense . 454	
Phyteuma orbiculare . 615	
spicatum . . 616	
Picris *arvalis* . 581	
echioides . 580	
hieracioides . 581	
Pilularia globulifera . 1267	
Pimpinella *dioica* . 408	
glauca . . 408	
magna . 418	
major . . 418	
Saxifraga . 417	
Pinguicula alpina . 665	
grandiflora . 664	
lusitanica . 666	
vulgaris . 664	
Pinus sylvestris . 936	
Pisum maritimum . 295	
Plantago Coronopus . 832	
intermedia . 828	
lanceolata . 830	

	FIG
major	828
maritima	831
media	829
Timbali	830
Platanthera *bifolia*	1006
solstitialis	1006
Poa alpina	1249
angustifolia	1245
annua	1243
aquatica	1236
Balfourii	1247
bulbosa	1250
cæsia	1247
compressa	1244
distans	1239
flexuosa	1248
fluitans	1237
glauca	1247
Kœleri	1246
laxa	1248
loliacea	1242
maritima	1238
minor	1248
montana	1247
nemoralis	1247
Parnellii	1247
parviflora	1246
polynoda	1244
pratensis	1245
procumbens	1240
rigida	1241
stricta	1248
strigosa	1245
sub-cœrulea	1245
sub compressa	1244
trivialis	1245
Polemonium cæruleum	685
Polistichum	
aculeatum	1288
Lonchitis	1287
Polycarpon	
tetraphyllum	173
Polygala *amara*	127
austriaca	127
calcarea	127
ciliata	127
depressa	127
grandiflora	127
oxyptera	127
serpyllacea	127
uliginosa	127
vulgaris	127
Polygonatum	
multiflorum	1031
officinale	1032
verticillatum	1030
Polygonum *agrestinum*	869
amphibium	875
arenastrum	869
aviculare	869
biforme	876
Bistorta	874
Convolvulus	871
dumetorum	872
Hydropiper	878
lapathifolium	877
laxum	877
littorale	869

	FIG
maculatum	877
maritimum	870
microspermum	869
minus	879
mite	879
nodosum	877
Persicaria	876
pseudodumetorum	871
Raii	870
Roberti	870
rurivagum	869
viviparum	873
Polypodium alpestre	1283
calcareum	1284
cambricum	1281
Dryopteris	1284
flexile	1283
Phegopteris	1282
Robertianum	1284
vulgare	1281
Polypogon littoralis	1182
monspeliensis	1181
Populus alba	933
canescens	933
fastigiata	935
glabra	934
nigra	935
tremula	934
villosa	934
Potamogeton	
acuminatus	960
acutifolius	966
compressus	965
crispus	963
cuspidatus	966
decipiens	960
densus	964
filiformis	968
flabellatus	968
fluitans	958
Friesii	967
gracilis	967
gramineus	965
Griffithii	961
heterophyllus	959
Jacksoni	960
juncifolius	968
lanceolatus	960
lithuanicus	961
Lonchites	960
longifolius	960
lucens	960
marinus	968
mucronatus	967
natans	958
nitens	959
oblongus	958
obtusifolius	965
pectinatus	968
perfoliatus	962
plantagineus	958
polygonifolius	958
prælongus	961
pusillus	967
rigida	967
rufescens	960
salicifolius	961
serratus	963

	FIG
spathulatus	960
Sturrockii	967
tenuissima	967
trichoides	967
Zizii	960
Zosterifolius	966
Potentilla *alpestris*	317
anserina	320
argentea	316
aurea	317
Comarum	327
Fragariastrum	313
fruticosa	319
maculata	317
mixta	314
nemoralis	315
norvegica	316
palustris	322
procumbens	315
reptans	314
rudens	317
rupestris	321
salisburgensis	317
Sibbaldi	318
Tormentilla	315
verna	317
Poterium *muricatum*	327
officinale	326
Sanguisorba	327
Prenanthes muralis	588
Primula *acaulis*	650
elatior	651
farinosa	652
officinalis	651
scotica	652
variabilis	651
veris	650
vulgaris	650
Prunella vulgaris	705
Prunus *Avium*	299
Cerasus	299
communis	298
domestica	298
insititia	298
Padus	300
spinosa	298
Psamma arenaria	1188
baltica	1188
Pseudathyrium	
alpestre	1283
Pteris aquilina	1308
Pulicaria dysenterica	518
vulgaris	519
Pulmonaria	
angustifolia	694
officinalis	694
Pyrethrum	
Parthenium	525
Pyrola *arenaria*	644
maritima	644
media	645
minor	646
rotundifolia	644
secunda	647
uniflora	643
Pyrus acerba	335
Achras	334
Aria	336

	FIG		FIG.		FIG
Aucuparia	338	*radians*	9	*concinna*	332
Briggsii	334	repens	18	*cordifolia*	330
communis	334	*reptans*	12	*corufolia*	332
cordata	334	*salsuginosus*	9	*coronata*	330
domestica	338	*Sardous*	21	*Crepiniana*	332
fennica	336	sceleratus	15	*cryptopoda*	331
germanica	341	*tomophyllus*	17	*decipiens*	332
hybrida	336	*trichophyllus*	9	*Doniana*	330
intermedia	336	*tripartitus*	10	*dumalis*	332
latifolia	336	*triphyllos*	9	*dumetorum*	332
Malus	335	*truncatus*	9	*Eglanteria*	331
mitis	335	*vulgaris*	9	*farinosa*	320
pinnatifida	336	*vulgatus*	17	*fastigiata*	533
Pyraster	334	Raphanus *maritimus*	113	*Forsteri*	332
rupicola	336	Raphanistrum	113	*frondosa*	332
scandica	336	Reseda alba	116	*gallicordes*	333
torminalis	337	*fruticulosa*	116	*glabra*	330
		Hookeri	116	*glaucophylla*	332
QUERCUS *intermedia*	917	lutea	115	*gracilescens*	330
pedunculata	917	luteola	114	*gracilis*	330
Robur	917	*suffruticulosa*	116	*Grovesii*	332
sessiliflora	917	Rhamnus catharticus	225	*Hailstonei*	332
		Frangula	226	*heterophylla*	330
RADIOLA *linoides*	194	Rhinanthus		*hibernica*	330
Millegrana	194	*angustifolius*	770	*Hystrix*	330
Ranunculus acris	17	aptera	770	*implexa*	332
apetalus	16	Crista-galli	770	*incana*	332
aquatilis	9	*major*	770	*inodora*	331
arvensis	23	*minor*	770	*involuta*	330
auricomus	16	*platyptena*	770	*Jundzilliana*	330
Bachii	9	*Reichenbachii*	770	*Kosinciana*	332
Baudotii	9	*stenoptera*	770	*lævigata*	330
Borœanus	17	*Rhodiola rosea*	361	*leucochroa*	333
bulbosus	20	Rhynchospora alba	1089	*lutetiana*	332
chœrophyllos	19	fusca	1088	*marginata*	332
circinatus	9	Ribes alpinum	374	*micrantha*	331
cœnosus	10	*Bromfieldiana*	373	*mollis*	330
confervoides	9	Grossularia	372	*mollissima*	330
confusus	9	nigrum	375	*monsoniæ*	333
depauperata	16	*petrœum*	373	*monticola*	332
divaricatus	9	rubrum	373	*Moorei*	330
divergens	14	*sativum*	373	*Nicholsoni*	330
diversifolius	9	*Smithiana*	373	*nivalis*	330
Drouetii	9	*spicatum*	373	*nuda*	332
Ficaria	14	*sylvestre*	373	*obovata*	330
fissifolius	9	*Uva-crispa*	372	*obtusifolia*	332
flabellatus	19	Rœmeria hybrida	43	*occidentalis*	330
Flammula	12	Romulea Columnæ	1021	*opaca*	333
floribundus	9	Rosa *agrestis*	331	*permixta*	331
fluitans	9	*Andevagensis*	332	pimpinellifolia	329
Godronii	9	*arvatica*	332	*platyphylla*	332
hederaceus	10	arvensis	333	*pomifera*	330
heterophyllus	9	*aspernata*	332	*pruinosa*	332
hirsutus	21	*Bakeri*	332	*Pseudo-rubiginosa*	330
homophyllus	10	*bibracteata*	333	*pulverulenta*	331
incumbens	14	*Billietii*	331	*repens*	333
intermedius	10	*biserrata*	332	*Reuteri*	332
Lenormandi	10	*Blondœana*	332	*Robertsoni*	330
Lingua	11	*Borreri*	332	*rubiginosa*	331
marinus	9	*bractescens*	332	*Sabini*	330
ophioglossifolius	13	*Briggsii*	331	*sarmentacea*	332
pantothryx	9	*britannica*	330	*scabriuscula*	330
parviflorus	22	*cœsia*	332	*sclerophylla*	332
parvulus	21	*canescens*	332	*scuticosa*	332
peltatus	9	canina	332	*sepium*	331
penicillatus	9	*celerata*	332	*Sherrardi*	330
peucedanifolius	9	*cœrulea*	330	*Smithii*	330
philonotis	21	*collina*	332	*sphœrica*	332
pseudo-fluitans	9				

	FIG		FIG.		FIG
spinonissima	329	*intermedius*	309	maritimus	865
stylosa	333	*Kœhleri*	308	*maximus*	861
subcristata	332	*latifolius*	308	*nemorosus*	863
subglobosa	330	*Leesii*	307	obtusifolius	860
surculosa	332	*Leightoni*	308	*palustris*	865
sylvestris	330	*Leightonianus*	308	*pratensis*	859
sylvicola	331	*Lejeunii*	308	pulcher	864
systyla	332	*lentiginosus*	308	*rupestris*	862
tomentella	332	*leucostachys*	308	sanguineus	863
tomentosa	330	*Lindleianus*	308	*Steinii*	865
uncinella	332	*macrophyllus*	308	*subcordata*	859
urbica	332	*menkii*	308	*sylvestris*	860
verticillacantha	332	*mucronatus*	308	*trigranulata*	859
villosa	330	*mucronulatus*	308	*viridis*	863
vinacea	332	*mutabilis*	308	Ruppia maritima	957
Watsoni	332	*nemorosus*	308	*nana*	957
Wilsoni	330	*nitidus*	308	*rostellata*	957
Woodsiana	330	*obliquus*	308	*spiralis*	957
Rubia peregrina	470	obtusifolius	307	Ruscus aculeatus	1036
tinctoria	470	*pallidus*	308		
Rubus *abruptus*	308	*pampinosus*	308	SAGINA *ambigua*	147
adscitus	308	*plicatus*	308	*apetala*	147
affinis	308	*præruptorum*	308	*ciliata*	147
althœifolius	308	*Pseudo-idœus*	309	*debilis*	147
amplificatus	308	*pubigera*	309	*densa*	147
Babingtonii	308	*Purchasii*	308	Linnæi	148
Balfourianus	308	*purpureus*	308	*maritima*	147
Bellardi	308	*pygmœus*	308	*nivalis*	148
Bloxami	308	*pyramidalis*	308	nodosa	149
Borreri	308	*Radula*	308	procumbens	147
Briggsii	308	*ramosus*	308	*saxatilis*	148
cæsius	309	*Reuteri*	308	*subulata*	148
calvatus	308	*rhamnifolius*	308	Sagittaria sagittifolia	973
carpinifolius	308	*rosaceus*	308	Salicornia herbacea	839
cavatifolius	308	*rotundifolius*	308	*lignosa*	839
Chamæmorus	311	*rubicolor*	309	*megastachya*	839
Colemanni	308	*rudis*	308	*procumbens*	839
concinnus	308	*Salteri*	308	*Pusilla*	839
conjungens	308	*Saltuum*	308	*Radicans*	839
cordifolius	308	saxatilis	310	*ramosissima*	839
corylifolius	308	*scaber*	308	Salix *acuminata*	923
dentatus	308	*Schlechtendahlii*	308	*acutifolia*	926
denticulatus	308	*Sprengelii*	308	alba	920
derasus	308	*suberectus*	308	*ambigua*	927
discolor	309	*sublustris*	308	amygdalina	921
diversifolius	308	*tenuis*	309	*Andersoniana*	926
dumetorum	308	*thyrsoideus*	308	*aquatica*	924
Emersistylus	308	*tuberculatus*	308	*Arbuscula*	930
fastigiatus	308	*ulmifolius*	309	*arbutifolia*	930
fissus	308	*umbrosus*	308	*arenaria*	927
foliosus	308	*vestitus*	308	*argentea*	927
fruticosus	308	*villicaulis*	308	*ascendens*	927
fusco-ater	308	*vulgaris*	308	*aurita*	925
fuscus	308	*Wahlbergii*	308	*Barreriana*	926
glabrata	308	Rumex Acetosa	866	*bicolor*	926
glandulosus	308	Acetosella	867	Caprea	924
Grabowskii	308	*acutus*	859	*carinata*	930
Guntheri	308	*alpinus*	858	*cinerea*	924
hemistemon	308	aquaticus	858	*cœrulea*	920
hirtifolius	308	conglomeratus	862	*contorta*	921
hirtus	308	*conspersus*	859	*cotinifolia*	926
hispidus	309	crispus	859	*Croweana*	926
humifusus	308	*elongatus*	859	*cuspidata*	918
Hystrix	308	*Friesii*	860	*damascena*	926
Idæus	307	Hydrolapathum	861	*daphnoides*	926
imbricatus	308	*Knafi*	865	*Davalliana*	926
incurvatus	308	*latifolia*	861	*decipiens*	919
infestus	308	*longifolius*	858	*Dicksoniana*	926

	FIG.
Doniana . . .	922
ferruginea . .	923
floribunda . .	926
foetida . .	927
Forbyana . .	922
Forsteriana . .	926
fragilis . .	919
fusca . .	927
glauca . .	923
Grahami . .	930
Helix . .	922
herbacea . .	932
hirta . .	926
Hoffmanniana .	921
holosericea . .	923
incubacea . .	927
lævis . .	930
Lambertiana . .	922
lanata . .	929
lanceolata . .	921
Laponum . .	928
laurina . .	926
laxiflora . .	926
livida . .	930
Meyeriana . .	918
mollissima . .	923
Myrsinites . .	930
myrtilloides . .	926
nigricans . .	926
nitens . .	926
oleifolia . .	924
parvifolia . .	927
pentandra . .	918
petræa . .	926
phillyreæfolia .	926
phylicifolia . .	926
pontederama . .	922
procumbens . .	930
propinqua . .	926
prostrata . .	927
prunifolia . .	930
purpurea . .	922
radicans . .	926
ramulosa . .	222
repens . .	927
reticulata . .	931
retusa . .	930
rosmarinifolia .	927
rubra . .	922
rugosa . .	923
rupestris . .	926
Russelliana . .	919
Sadleri . .	929
serrata . .	930
Smithiana . .	923
spathulata . .	924
sphacelata . .	924
stipularis . .	926
Stuartiana . .	928
tenuifolia . .	926
tenuior . .	926
tetrapla . .	926
Trevirani . .	921
triandra . .	921
undulata . .	921
vaciniifolia . .	930
venulosa . .	930
versifolia . .	927

	FIG.
viminalis . .	923
viridis . .	919
vitellina . .	920
Weigeliana . .	926
Woolgariana . .	922
Wulfeniana . .	926
Salsola Kali .	842
Salvia pratensis . .	777
Verbenaca . .	778
Sambucus Ebulus .	463
nigra . .	462
Samolus Valerandi .	663
Sanguisorba officinalis .	326
Sanicula europæa .	399
Saponaria *hybrida* .	133
officinalis . .	133
puberula . .	133
Sarothamnus scoparius	232
Saussurea alpina .	557
Saxifraga *affinis* .	379
aizoides . .	377
autumnalis . .	377
cæspitosa . .	380
cernua . .	382
condensata . .	379
decipiens . .	379
elegans . .	387
elongata . .	379
gemmifera . .	379
Geum . .	388
gracilis . .	387
granulata . .	381
greenlandica . .	380
hibernica . .	379
Hirculus . .	378
hirsuta . .	387
hirta . .	379
hypnoides . .	379
incurvifolia . .	380
integrifolia . .	386
læte-virens . .	379
lævis . .	379
leptophylla . .	379
nivalis . .	385
oppositifolia . .	376
palmata . .	379
platypetala . .	379
punctata . .	387
quinquefida . .	379
rivularis . .	383
serratifolia . .	387
sponhemica . .	379
stellaris . .	386
Sternbergii . .	379
tridactylites . .	384
trifida . .	379
umbrosa . .	387
Scabiosa arvensis .	496
Columbaria . .	495
succisa . .	494
Scandix *Anthriscus* .	446
cerefolium . .	445
Pecten . .	441
Scheuchzeria palustris .	969
Schoberia fruticosa .	840
maritima . .	841
Schœnus ferrugineus .	1086
nigricans . .	1085

	FIG.
Scilla autumnalis .	1045
nutans . .	1046
verna . .	1044
Scirpus acicularis .	1092
cæspitosus . .	1097
caricinus . .	1090
Caricis . .	1090
carinatus . .	1104
Davalii . .	1104
fluitans . .	1098
glaucus . .	1104
Holoschœnus . .	1101
lacustris . .	1104
maritimus . .	1105
multicaulis . .	1095
palustris . .	1094
parvulus . .	1093
pauciflorus . .	1096
planifolius . .	1090
pungens . .	1102
pygmæus . .	1100
riparius . .	1100
Rothii . .	1102
rufus . .	1091
Savii . .	1100
setaceus . .	1099
sylvaticus . .	1106
Tabernœmontani .	1104
triqueter . .	1103
uniglumis . .	1094
Watsoni . .	1094
Scleranthus annuus .	837
biennis . .	837
perennis . .	838
Sclerochloa Borreri .	1239
conferta . .	1239
distans . .	1239
loliacea . .	1242
maritima . .	1238
multicaulis . .	1239
procumbens . .	1240
rigida . .	1241
Scolopendrium vulgare	1305
Scrophularia aquatica .	748
Balbisii . .	743
cinerea . .	743
Ehrharti . .	748
nodosa . .	742
Scorodonia . .	744
umbrosa . .	743
vernalis . .	745
Scutellaria galericulata	796
minor . .	797
Sedum acre . .	367
albescens . .	369
album . .	365
anglicum . .	363
dasyphyllum . .	364
elegans . .	369
Fabaria . .	362
Forsterianum . .	369
glaucum . .	370
micranthum . .	365
pruinatum . .	369
purpurascens . .	362
reflexum . .	370
Rhodiola . .	361
rupestre . .	369

	FIG.
sexangulare . .	368
tectorum . . .	870
Telephium . .	362
teretifolium .	365
villosum . .	366
Selaginella selaginoides	1264
spinosa .	1264
Sempervivum tectorum	371
Senebiera Coronopus .	108
didyma . .	109
Senecio aquaticus .	546
barbareæfolius .	546
campestris .	552
erraticus . .	546
erucifolius .	548
flosculosus .	547
Jacobæa . .	547
lividus . .	544
maritima . .	552
paludosus .	549
palustris . .	551
radiata . .	542
saracenicus .	550
spathulæfolius .	552
squalidus . .	545
sylvaticus . .	544
tenuifolius .	548
viscosus . .	543
vulgaris . .	542
Serrafalcus arvensis .	1224
Serratula tinctoria .	556
Seseli Libanotis .	429
Sesleria cærulea .	1257
Setaria glauca .	1163
verticillata .	1162
viridis .	1164
Sherardia arvensis .	483
Sibbaldia procumbens	318
Sibthorpia europæa .	748
Sieglingia decumbens .	1255
Silaus pratensis .	431
Silene acaulis . .	134
anglica . .	138
conica . .	139
Cucubalus . .	135
gallica . .	138
inflata . .	135
maritima . .	135
noctiflora . .	140
nutans . .	137
Otites . .	136
paradoxa . .	137
puberula .	135
quinquevulnera .	138
Silybum mariamum .	558
Simethis bicolor .	1056
planifolia . .	1056
Sinapis alba .	81
arvensis . .	82
Cheiranthus .	78
incana . .	84
nigra . .	83
tenuifolia .	76
Sison Amomum .	407
Sisymbrium *alliaria* .	73
Irio . .	71
murale . .	77
officinale . .	70

	FIG.
Sophia . . .	72
tenuifolium . .	76
Thaliana . .	61
Sisyrinchium	
angustifolium .	1020
bermudiana .	1020
Sium angustifolium .	416
erectum . .	416
latifolium . .	415
repens . .	405
Smilacina bifolia .	1034
Smyrnium Olusatrum .	455
Solanum Dulcamara .	715
luteo-virescens .	716
marimum . .	715
minuatum . .	716
nigrum . .	716
Solidago *angustifolia* .	503
cambrica . .	503
Virga-aurea .	503
Sonchus *alpinus* .	591
arvensis . .	592
asper . .	594
cæruleus . .	591
glabra . .	592
oleraceus . .	594
palustris . .	593
Sorbus fennica .	336
latifolia . .	336
scandica . .	336
Sparganium *affine* .	942
minimum . .	943
natans . .	942
ramosum . .	941
simplex . .	942
Spartina *alterniflora* .	1205
stricta . .	1205
Townsendii .	1205
Spartium scoparium .	232
Specularia hybrida .	625
Spergula arvensis .	172
nodosa . .	149
saginoides . .	148
sativa . .	172
stricta . .	152
subulata . .	148
vulgaris . .	172
Spergularia *marina* .	171
media . .	171
rubra . .	171
rupestris . .	171
salina . .	171
Spiræa Filipendula .	303
salicifolia . .	301
Ulmaria . .	302
Spiranthes æstivalis .	994
autumnalis .	993
cernua . .	995
gemmipara . .	995
Romanzoviana .	995
Stachys *ambigua* .	803
arvensis . .	804
Betonica . .	800
germanica . .	801
palustris . .	803
sylvatica . .	802
Statice *Armeria* .	826
auriculæfolia .	824

	FIG.
bahusiensis . .	823
Behen . .	823
bellidifolia . .	825
binervosa . .	824
Caspia . .	824
Dodartii . .	824
intermedia . .	824
Limonium . .	823
occidentalis . .	824
oxylepis . .	824
rariflora . .	823
reticulata . .	825
serotina . .	823
spathulata . .	824
Stellaria aquatica .	164
Boræana .	166
cerastoides .	163
Elizabethæ .	166
glauca . .	169
graminea . .	168
Holostea . .	170
media . .	166
neglecta . .	166
nemorum . .	165
palustris . .	169
scapigera . .	168
uliginosa . .	167
umbrosa . .	166
Stratiotes aloides .	980
Sturmia Loeselii .	982
minima . .	1179
Suæda *chenopodina* .	841
fruticosa . .	840
maritima . .	841
Subularia aquatica .	95
Symphytum officinale	707
patens . .	707
tuberosum . .	708
TAMARIX *anglica* .	176
gallica . .	176
Tamus communis .	1028
Tanacetum vulgare .	535
Taraxacum Dens-leonis	595
Erythrospermum .	595
lævigatum .	595
officinale . .	595
palustre . .	595
Taxus baccata .	938
fastigiata . .	938
Teesdalia *Iberis* .	99
nudicaulis . .	99
Teucrium Botrys .	817
Chamædrys .	818
scordioides .	816
Scordium . .	816
Scorodonia . .	815
Thalictrum alpinum .	2
calcareum . .	3
dunense . .	3
flavum . .	4
flexuosum . .	3
Kochii . .	3
majus . .	3
minus . .	3
montanum . .	3
Morisonii . .	4
riparium . .	4

	FIG.
saxatile . . .	3
sphærocarpum . .	4
Thesium *anglicum* .	883
divaricatum .	883
humifusum .	883
linophyllum .	883
Thlaspi alpestre . .	98
arvense . .	96
occitanum . .	98
perfoliatum .	97
sylvestre . .	98
virens . .	98
Thrincia hirta .	583
Thymus *Acinos* .	790
Chamædrys .	788
Serpyllum .	788
Tilia *cordata* .	201
europæa .	201
grandifolia .	201
intermedia .	201
parvifolia . .	201
platyphyllos .	201
vulgaris . .	201
Tillæa muscosa .	359
Tinia cylindracea .	1008
intacta . .	1008
Tofieldia *borealis* .	1058
palustris . .	1058
Tordylium maximum .	440
Torilis Anthriscus .	448
infesta . .	449
nodosa . .	447
Tormentilla erecta .	315
officinalis . .	315
reptans . .	315
Tragopogon *grandiflora*	578
minor . .	578
porrifolius .	579
pratensis . .	578
Trichomanes	
Andrewsii .	1313
brevisetum .	1313
radicans .	1313
speciosum .	1313
Trichonema	
bulbocodium .	1021
Columnæ .	1021
Trientalis europæa .	658
Trifolium arvense .	246
Bocconi . .	253
dubium . .	264
elegans . .	255
erecta . .	252
filiforme . .	265
fragiferum . .	260
glomeratum .	256
hybridum .	262
incarnatum .	245
maritimum .	251
medium . .	250
minus . .	264
Molineri . .	245
ochroleucum .	248
ornithopedioides .	244
parviflora . .	249
pratense . .	249
procumbens .	263
repens . .	261

	FIG
resupinatum . .	258
sativum . .	249
scabrum . .	254
squarrosum . .	251
stellatum . .	247
striatum . .	252
strictum . .	255
subterraneum .	259
suffocatum .	257
Townsendi . .	261
Triglochin maritimum	971
palustre . .	970
Trigonella	
ornithopodioides .	244
purpurascens . .	244
Trinia vulgaris . .	408
Triodia decumbens .	1255
Trisetum flavescens .	1200
Triticum acutum .	1213
alpinum . .	1213
biflora . .	1213
caninum . .	1214
junceum . .	1213
laxum . .	1213
littorale . .	1213
loliaceum . .	1227
pungens . .	1213
repens . .	1213
Trollius europæus .	25
Tulipa sylvestris . .	1038
Tunica prolifer . .	129
Turritis glabra . .	56
hirsuta . .	58
Tussilago Farfara .	540
hybrida . .	541
Petasites . .	541
Typha angustifolia .	940
latifolia . .	939
media . .	939
Udora canadensis .	978
Ulex europæus . .	227
Gallii . .	228
nanus . .	228
strictus . .	227
Ulmus campestris .	909
campestris . .	908
carpinifolia . .	909
glabra . .	909
major . .	908
montana . .	908
stricta . .	909
suberosa . .	909
Urtica dioica . .	905
Dodartii . .	904
pilulifera . .	904
urens . .	903
Utricularia *Bremii* .	668
intermedia . .	669
minor . .	668
neglecta . .	667
vulgaris . .	667
VACCINIUM Myrtillus	626
Oxycoccos .	629
uliginosum .	627
Vitis-idæa . .	628
Valantia cruciata .	471
Valeriana dioica . .	485

	FIG.
Locusta . . .	488
micani . .	486
officinalis . .	486
pyrenaica . .	487
sambucifolia . .	486
Valerianella Auricula	490
carinata . .	489
dentata . .	491
eriocarpa . .	491
mixta . .	491
Morisonii . .	491
olitoria . .	488
rimosa . .	490
tridentata . .	490
Verbascum Blattaria .	727
Lychnitis . .	730
nigrum . .	729
pulverulentum .	731
thapsiforme . .	726
Thapsus . .	726
tomentosum .	729
virgatum . .	728
Verbena officinalis .	822
Veronica agrestis .	761
alpina . .	752
Anagallis . .	755
arvensis . .	763
Beccabunga .	756
Buxbaumii .	762
Chamædrys .	759
eximia . .	763
fruticulosa . .	751
hederæfolia .	760
hirsuta . .	754
humifusa . .	753
hybrida . .	750
montana . .	758
officinalis . .	754
opaca . .	761
perpusilla . .	761
persica . .	762
polita . .	761
saligna . .	754
saxatilis . .	751
scutellata . .	757
serpyllifolia .	753
spicata . .	750
triphyllos . .	765
verna . .	764
Viburnum Lantana .	464
Opulus . .	465
Vicia *angustifolia* .	285
bithynica . .	287
Bobartii . .	285
Cracca . .	280
gemella . .	279
gracilis . .	279
hirsuta . .	278
hybrida . .	284
lævigata . .	234
lathyroides .	286
lutea . .	234
Orobus . .	282
sativa . .	285
segetalis . .	285
sepium . .	283
sylvatica . .	281
tetrasperma .	279

	FIG.
Villarsia nymphœoides	684
reniformis	684
Vinca major	672
minor	673
Viola	
amœna	126
arenaria	124
arvensis	126
calcarea	123
canina	125
Curtisii	126
flavicornis	125
Fosteri	126
grandiflora	126
hamulata	126
hirta	123
lactea	125
lutea	126
Mackaii	126
odorata	122

	FIG.
palustris	121
permixta	122
persicæfolia	125
pumila	125
Reichenbachiana	125
Riviniana	125
sabulosa	126
sepincola	122
stagnina	125
sylvatica	125
Symei	126
tricolor	126
Viscum album	458
Vulpia membranacea	1230
Myurus	1229
uniglumis	1230
Wahlenbergia	
hederacia	624
Wolffia arrhiza	950

	FIG.
Woodsia *hyperborea*	1312
ilvensis	1312
XANTHIUM	
spinosum	520
Strumarium	520
ZANNICHELLIA	
brachystemon	956
macrostemon	956
major	956
palustris	956
pedicellata	956
pedunculata	956
polycarpa	956
tenuissima	956
Zostera *angustifolia*	951
marina	951
nana	952

Y

INDEX

OF

ENGLISH AND POPULAR NAMES.

	FIG		FIG.		FIG
ABELE . . . 933		Sea . . . 537		Bilberry . . . 626	
Absinth . . . 539		Wormwood . . 539		Bindweed, Black . 871	
Aconite . . . 30		Arum . . . 944		Larger . . . 687	
Adder's tongue . . 1278		Asarabacca . . 884		Lesser . . . 686	
Agrimony, Common . 328		Ash, Common . . 670		Sea . . . 688	
Hemp . . . 497		Mountain . . 338		Birch, Common . 912	
Agropyrum, Couch . 1213		Asparagus . . 1035		Dwarf . . . 913	
Fibrous . . 1214		Aspen . . . 934		Bird's-foot, Common 275	
Agrostis, Bristle . 1185		Asphodel, Bog . 1057		Sand . . . 274	
Silky . . 1186		Lancashire . 1057		Trefoil . . 266	
Aira, Early . . 1196		Scottish . . 1058		Bird's-nest, Yellow . 648	
Grey . . . 1195		Aster, Sea . . 498		Bishopweed . . . 409	
Silvery . . 1197		Astragal, Alpine . 270		Bistort . . . 874	
Tufted . . 1193		Purple . . 269		Bittercress, Bulbiferous 68	
Wavy . . 1194		Astrantia, Larger . 400		Hairy . . . 67	
Alchemil, Alpine . 324		Avens, Common . 305		Large . . . 64	
Common . . 323		Water . . 306		Meadow . . 65	
Field . . . 325		Awlwort . . . 95		Narrow-leaved . 66	
Alder, Berry-bearing 226				Bittersweet.. . . 715	
Common . . 911		BALDMONEY . . 432		Blackberry . . . 308	
Alexanders . . 455		Ballota, Black . 808		Blackthorn . . 298	
Alkanet, Bastard . 696		Balm . . . 798		Bladderfern, Brittle . 1310	
Common . . 704		Balsam, Orange . 220		Mountain . . 1311	
Green . . 705		Yellow . . 219		Bladder-seed . . 454	
Allgood . . . 851		Baneberry . . 31		Bladderwort, Common 667	
All-heal . . . 486		Barberry . . . 33		Intermediate . 669	
Allseed . . . 194		Barley, Meadow . 1210		Lesser . . . 668	
Althæa, Hispid . 200		Sea . . . 1212		Blaeberry . . . 626	
Marsh . . 199		Wall . . . 1211		Blechnum . . . 1307	
Alyssum, Small . 87		Wood . . . 1209		Blinks . . . 175	
Sweet . . 88		Bartsia, Alpine . 766		Bluebell . . . 1046	
Andromeda, Marsh 633		Red . . . 768		Bluebottle . . 574	
Anemone, Pasque . 5		Viscid . . 767		Blue-eyed Grass . 1020	
Wood . . . 6		Basil, Wild . . 792		Blysmus, Broad . 1090	
Angelica, Wild . 434		Beaksedge, Brown . 1088		Narrow . . 1091	
Antennaria, Mountain 512		White . . 1089		Bog Bean . . . 683	
Pearl . . 513		Beam-tree . . 336		Myrtle . . 910	
Anthoxanth . . 1167		Bearberry, Black . 632		Rush. . . . 1085	
Apium, Lesser . 406		Common . . 631		Borage . . . 709	
Procumbent . 405		Beardgrass, Annual 1181		Borecole . . . 79	
Apple, Wild or Crab 335		Perennial . 1182		Box 899	
Arbutus . . . 630		Bear's-foot . . 26		Brake or Bracken . 1308	
Archangel, Yellow . 814		Beech . . . 916		Rock . . . 1285	
Arnoseris, Dwarf . 610		Beech Fern . . 1282		Bramble . . 308	
Arrow-grass, Marsh . 970		Beet . . . 852		Brandy-bottle . . 35	
Sea . . . 971		Belladonna . . 717		Brassica, Field . 80	
Arrowhead . . 973		Bergamot . . . 784		Hoary . . . 84	
Artimisia, Common . 538		Betony . . . 800		Isle of Man . 78	
Field . . 536		Bidens, Three-cleft . 522		Sand . . . 77	

	FIG.
Wall	76
Bristle Fern	1313
Broccoli	79
Brome, Barren	1221
Compact	1223
Field	1224
Great	1222
Hairy	1220
Tall	1225
Upright	1219
Brooklime	756
Brookweed	663
Broom, Butcher's	1036
Common	232
Broomrape, Blue	723
Branched	724
Clove-scented	719
Great	718
Lesser	722
Red	720
Tall	721
Brussels sprouts	79
Bryony, Black	1028
Common	358
Buckbean	683
Buckthorn, Alder	226
Common	225
Sea	882
Bugle, Creeping	819
Erect	820
Yellow	821
Bugloss, Small	706
Viper's	692
Bullace	298
Bulrush	1104
Buplever, Falcate	422
Hare's-ear	419
Narrow	420
Slender	421
Burdock	555
Bur-Marigold	521
-Parsley	450
-reed	941
Burnet, Garden	327
Great	326
Salad	327
Saxifrage	417
Burweed	520
Butcher's Broom	1036
Butterbur	541
Buttercup	17
Butterwort, Alpine	665
Common	664
Pale	666
Butome	972
CABBAGE	79
St. Patrick's	387
Calamint, Common	791
Field	790
Hedge	792
Callitriche	902
Cameline	94
Campanula, Clustered	617
Corn	625
Creeping	620
Giant	619
Harebell	623

	FIG.
Ivy	624
Nettle-leaved	618
Rampion	621
Spreading	622
Campion, Bladder	135
Moss	134
Canary-grass	1168
Candytuft, Bitter	100
Caper-spurge	892
Capsell	102
Caraway	413
Carex, Acute	1130
Alpine	1131
Axillary	1121
Black	1133
Bladder	1156
Bottle	1155
Buxbaum's	1132
Capillary	1148
Carnation	1147
Curved	1127
Cyperus like	1153
Diœcious	1111
Distant	1145
Divided	1126
Dotted	1146
Downy	1139
Dwarf	1134
Elongated	1117
Few-flowered	1114
Fingered	1135
Flea	1112
Fox	1123
Glaucous	1150
Hairy	1141
Hare's-foot	1116
Longbracted	1143
Marsh	1157
Mountain	1137
Mud	1149
Oval	1115
Pale	1142
Panicled	1122
Pendulous	1154
Pill headed	1138
Prickly	1124
Remote	1110
Rock	1113
Russet	1128
Sand	1125
Slender	1140
Star headed	1118
Thin-spiked	1152
Tufted	1129
Vernal	1136
Whitish	1119
Wood	1151
Yellow	1144
Carline	571
Carnation	132
Carrot	452
Carum, Caraway	413
Corn	411
Parsley	410
Tuberous	414
Whorled	412
Catabrose, Water	1251
Catchfly, Nottingham	137

	FIG.
Catmint	794
Cat's-ear	512, 586
Cat's-foot	512
Cat's-tail	939, 1170
Caucalis, Broad	451
Knotted	447
Small	450
Spreading	449
Cauliflower	79
Celandine, Common	42
Lesser	14
Celery	404
Centaurea, Greater	573
Guernsey	575
Yellow	577
Centaury	676
Centranth	484
Centuncle	662
Cerast, Alpine	162
Common	160
Field	161
Starwort	163
Ceterach	1306
Chaffweed	662
Chamagrostis, Dwarf	1179
Chamomile, Common	530
Corn	529
Fetid	528
Wild	527
Yellow	531
Charlock	82
Jointed	113
White	113
Cherry, Bird	300
Dwarf or Wild	299
Chervil, Burr	446
Rough	444
Wild	445
Chickweed	166
Mouse-ear	160
Water	175
Chicory	609
Chives	1051
Christopher, Herb	31
Chrysanthemum, Corn	524
Feverfew	525
Oxeye	523
Chrysosplene,	
Alternate-leaved	389
Opposite-leaved	388
Cicely, Sweet	442
Cicendia, Dwarf	675
Slender	674
Cinquefoil	314
Circæa, Alpine	354
Common	353
Cladium, Prickly	1087
Clary	778
Claytonia, Perfoliate	174
Cleavers	479
Clematis	1
Cloudberry	311
Clover, Alsike	262
Boccone's	253
Clustered	256
Crimson	245
Dutch	261
Hare's-foot	246

	FIG.
Hop . . .	263
Knotted . .	252
Lesser . .	264
Meadow . .	250
Purple . .	249
Red . .	249
Reversed . .	258
Rough . .	254
Sea . .	251
Slender . .	265
Starry . .	247
Strawberry .	260
Subterranean .	259
Suffocated .	257
Sulphur . .	248
Upright . .	255
White . .	261
Zigzag . .	250
Clubmoss, Alpine	1261
Common . .	1259
Fir . .	1262
Interrupted .	1260
Lesser . .	1264
Marsh . .	1263
Club-rush . .	939
Cock's-foot .	1231
Codlins-and-cream	343
Colchicum .	1059
Cole-rabi . .	79
Coltsfoot . .	540
Columbine . .	28
Colza . .	80
Comfrey, Common	707
Tuberous .	708
Conopodium .	443
Coralroot . .	68
Spurless . .	983
Cordgrass . .	1205
Coriander . .	456
Corn Cockle .	143
Flower . .	574
Marigold . .	524
Cornel Dwarf .	459
Cornsalad, Common	488
Keeled . .	489
Narrow-fruited	491
Sharp-fruited .	490
Corydal, Climbing	47
Yellow . .	46
Cotoneaster . .	340
Cotton grass or sedge,	
Alpine . .	1107
Common . .	1109
Sheathing .	1108
Weed . .	534
Couch . .	1213
Cowbane . .	403
Cowberry . .	628
Cow-parsnip .	439
Cowslip . .	651
Cowwheat, Common	775
Crested . .	773
Purple . .	774
Small-flowered .	776
Crab apple . .	335
Cranberry . .	629
Crane's-bill . .	202
Creeping Jenny .	656

	FIG.
Crepis, Beaked .	596
Fetid . .	597
Hawkweed .	600
Marsh . .	601
Rough . .	599
Smooth . .	598
Cress, Hoary .	105
Narrow-leaved .	107
Sea . .	111
Smith's . .	104
Crocus, Autumnal	1023
Spring or purple	1022
Crosswort . .	471
Crowberry . .	900
Crowfoot . .	17
Crow Garlic . .	1053
Cuckoo-flower .	65
Pint . .	944
Cudweed . .	505
Dwarf . .	510
Jersey . .	508
Marsh . .	511
Wood . .	509
Currant, Black .	375
Mountain .	376
Red and White .	373
Cyclamen . .	653
Cynodon, Creeping	1203
Cyperus, Brown .	1084
Cyphel . . .	150
DAFFODIL . .	1024
Daffy-down-dilly .	1024
Daisy, Common .	504
Oxeye . .	523
Damasonium, Star	977
Dame's Violet .	69
Damson . .	298
Dandelion . .	595
Danewort . .	463
Darnel . .	1216
Deadly Nightshade .	717
Dead-nettle, Red .	811
Spotted . .	813
White . .	812
Devil's-bit . .	494
Dewberry . .	309
Dittander . .	106
Dock, Broad .	860
Clustered . .	862
Curled . .	859
Fiddle . .	864
Golden . .	865
Red-veined .	863
Smooth-fruited .	858
Sorrel . .	866
Water . .	861
Dodder, Flax .	690
Greater . .	689
Lesser . .	691
Dogberry . .	460
Dog's Mercury .	897
Dog's-tail, Crested	1232
Rough . .	1233
Dog-rose . .	332
Dogwood . .	460
Doronic, Plantain	554
Dove's-foot . .	212

	FIG.
Draba, Hoary .	91
Rock . .	90
Wall . .	92
Yellow . .	89
Dropwort . .	303
Water . .	423
Dryas, White .	304
Duckweed, Gibbous	948
Greater .	949
Ivy-leaved .	946
Lesser . .	947
Rootless . .	950
Dutch Rush . .	1275
Dwale . .	717
Dyer's Rocket .	114
Weed . .	114
Woad . .	110
EARTHNUT . .	443
Echium, Purple .	693
Elatine, Eight-stamened	178
Six-stamened .	177
Elder, Common .	462
Dwarf . .	463
Elecampane .	514
Elm, Common .	909
Mountain .	908
Scotch . .	908
Wych . .	908
Elodia, Canadian .	978
Enchanter's	
Nightshade .	353
Epilobe, Alpine .	350
Broad-leaved .	345
Chickweed .	349
Great . .	343
Hoary . .	344
Marsh . .	348
Pale . .	346
Square . .	347
Willow . .	342
Epipactis, Broad	984
Marsh . .	985
Epipogum, Leafless .	992
Equisetum, Bog .	1273
Field . .	1269
Great . .	1268
Long . .	1276
Marsh . .	1274
Rough . .	1275
Shady . .	1271
Smooth . .	1272
Wood . .	1270
Variegated .	1277
Erigeron, Alpine .	501
Canadian .	502
Eriocaulon, Jointed	1082
Erodium, Common .	214
Musk . .	215
Sea . .	216
Eryngo, Field .	402
Sea . .	401
Eupatory . .	497
Evening Primrose .	351
Everlasting, Mountain	512
Eyebright . .	769
FALSE-BROME, Heath .	1218

	FIG.
Slender	1217
False-Oat	1200
Featherfoil	649
Felwort	680
Fennel, Common	428
Hog's	435
Water	9
Fenugreek	244
Fern, Adder's tongue	1278
Beech	1282
Bladder	1310
Bristle	1313
Filmy	1314
Hard	1307
Hart's-tongue	1305
Holly	1287
Lady	1295
Maidenhair	1309
Male	1291
Marsh	1289
Oak	1284
Parsley	1285
Royal	1280
Fescue, Meadow	1227
One-glumed	1230
Rat's tail	1229
Reed	1228
Sheep's	1226
Fever-few	525
Figwort	742
Filago, Field	506
Narrow	507
Filmy Fern	1314
Fiorin grass	1183
Fir, Scotch	936
Flag, Sweet	945
Yellow	1017
Flax, Cathartic	193
Common	190
Pale	192
Perennial	191
Purging	193
Flax-seed	194
Fleabane	502, 518
Small	519
Flixweed	72
Fool's Parsley	427
Forget me-not	699
Foxglove, Purple	749
Foxtail, Alpine	1178
Marsh	1177
Meadow	1176
Slender	1175
French Willow	342
Fritillary	1037
Frogbit	979
Fuller's herb	133
Fumitory, Common	45
Furze, Common	227
Dwarf	228
Irish	227
Needle	231
GAGEA, Yellow	1040
Gale, Sweet	910
Galeopsis, Common	807
Downy	806
Red	805

	FIG
Galingale	1083
Galium, Corn	480
Heath	475
Hedge	476
Marsh	473
Northern	478
Swamp	474
Wall	477
Garlic, Crow	1053
Field	1050
Mustard	73
Gean	299
Genista, Dyer's	229
Hairy	230
Needle	231
Gentian, Autumn	680
Field	681
Marsh	677
Small	679
Spring	678
Geraneum, Blood-red	202
Cut-leaved	*212
Dove's foot	209
Dusky	203
Herb-Robert	207
Long-stalked	213
Meadow	205
Mountain	206
Round-leaved	211
Shining	208
Small-flowered	210
Wood	204
Germander, Cut-leaved	817
Wall	818
Water	816
Wood	815
Gilliflower	48
Gipsywort	779
Gladdon	1018
Gladiolus	1019
Glasswort	839
Globeflower	25
Goat's-beard, Yellow	578
Goldenrod	503
Goldilocks	16, 449
Gold of Pleasure	94
Gontweed	409
Good King Henry	851
Goodyera, Creeping	996
Gooseberry, Wild	372
Goosefoot, Glaucus	846
Many-seeded	844
Maple-leaved	850
Nettle-leaved	849
Red	847
Stinking	843
Upright	848
White	845
Goosegrass	479
Gorse	227
Goutweed	409
Grammites, Small	1286
Grape Hyacinth	1047
Grass, Beard	1181, 1182
Bent	1184
Bermuda	1204
Blue-eyed	1020
Canary	1168

	FIG.
Carnation	1146
Cock's-foot	1231
Cord	1205
Couch	1213
Dog's-tail	1232, 1233
Dog's-tooth	1204
Fescue	1226–1230
Fiorin	1183
Hair	1196
Holy	1166
Lyme	1208
Manna	1236–1241
Maram	1188
Meadow	1245
Millet	1159
Nit	1187
of Parnassus	391
Quake	1234, 1235
Quitch	1213
Reed	1169
Rye	1215
Scorpion	699–703
Squirrel-tail	1212
Timothy	1169
Vernal	1167
Grass-wrack	951
Dwarf	952
Great Burnet	326
Great Willow-herb	343
Greek Valerian	685
Greenwood	229
Gromwell, Common	697
Corn	696
Creeping	698
Ground-Ivy	793
Pine	821
Groundsel	542
Guelder-Rose	465
Guimauve	199
HABENARIA, Butterfly	1006
Dense-spiked	1008
Fragrant	1007
Green	1010
Small	1009
Hair-grass	1197
Hardheads	572
Harebell	623
Hare's Ear	75, 419
Hare's-tail	1180
Hart's-tongue	1305
Hartwort, Great	440
Hautboy	312
Hawkbit, Autumnal	583
Common	582
Lesser	584
Hawk's-beard	596–601
Hawkweed, Alpine	603
Honeywort	605
Mouse-ear	602
Prenanth	608
Savoy	607
Umbellate	606
Wall	604
Hawthorn	339
Hazel	915
Heartsease	126
Heath, Ciliated	639

	FIG.
Cornish . . .	641
Cross-leaved . .	638
Mediterranean. .	640
Sea . . .	128
St. Dabeoc's .	635
Heather, Bell . .	637
Hedge Mustard . .	70
Parsley . . .	448
Hellebore, Fetid .	27
Green . . .	26
Helleborine, Narrow .	987
Red . . .	985
White . . .	986
Hemlock, Common .	453
Water . . .	403
Hemp Agrimony . .	497
Nettle . . .	807
Henbane . . .	714
Henbit . . .	810
Heracleum . . .	439
Herb-Bennet . .	305
Herb, Christopher .	31
Gerard . . .	409
Paris . . .	1029
Robert . . .	207
Hippocrepis . .	276
Hog's Fennel . .	435
Hogweed . . .	439
Holcus, Woolly . .	1202
Soft . . .	1203
Holly, Common .	223
Sea . . .	401
Holly Fern . . .	1287
Holosteum, Umbellate	159
Holygrass, Northern .	1166
Honewort . . .	408
Honeysuckle, Common .	466
Fly . . .	468
Perfoliate . .	467
Hop . . .	907
Horehound, Black .	808
White . . .	799
Hornbeam . . .	914
Hornwort . . .	901
Horseradish . .	85
Horsetail . . .	1269
Hound's Tongue,	
Common . .	711
Green . . .	712
Houseleek . . .	371
Hutchinsia, Rock .	101
Hyacinth, Grape . .	1047
Wild . . .	1046
Hypericum, Common .	181
Flax-leaved . .	185
Hairy . . .	187
Imperforate . .	182
Large-flowered .	179
Marsh . . .	189
Mountain . .	188
Slender . . .	186
Square-stalked .	183
Trailing . . .	184
Tutsan . . .	180
Hypochœre, Glabrous	585
Spotted . . .	587
ILLECEBRUM . .	836

	FIG
Inule, Fleabane .	518
Willow-leaved	515
Iris, Fetid . .	1018
Yellow . .	1017
Ivy, Common . .	457
Ground . .	793
JACK-BY-THE-HEDGE .	73
Jacob's Ladder . .	685
Juniper . . .	937
KALE . . .	79
Kidney Vetch .	268
Knapweed . . .	572
Knawel, Annual	837
Perennial . .	838
Knotgrass . . .	869
Knotweed . . .	869
Kobresia . . .	1110
Kœleria, Crested .	1256
Kohlrabbi . . .	79
LADY Fern . .	1295
Lady's Bedstraw .	472
Fingers . .	268
Mantle . . .	323
Slipper . .	1016
Smock . .	65
Tresses . 993, 994, 995	
Lamb's Lettuce . .	488
Succory . .	610
Lapsane . . .	611
Larkspur . . .	29
Laurel, Spurge . .	881
Lavender, Sea . .	823
Leek, Field . .	1050
Round-headed .	1052
Sand . . .	1049
Triquetrous .	1055
Wild . . .	1048
Leersia . . .	1158
Lent Lily . . .	1024
Leopard's-bane . .	553
Lepturus, Curved .	1206
Lettuce, Alpine . .	591
Prickly . .	589
Wall . . .	588
Willow . . .	590
Lily, Lent . . .	1024
Lily-of-the-Valley .	1033
Lime-tree . . .	201
Limnanth . . .	684
Limosel . . .	747
Linaria, Common .	734
Ivy . . .	739
Lesser . . .	738
Pale . . .	735
Pellisser's . .	736
Pointed . .	741
Round-leaved .	740
Supine . . .	737
Ling . . .	642
Linnæa . . .	469
Linseed . . .	190
Liparis, Two-leaved .	982
Littorel . . .	833
Livelong . . .	362
Lloydia, Mountain .	1039
Lobelia, Acrid . .	613

	FIG
Water . . .	612
Loiseleuria . . .	634
London Pride . .	387
London Rocket . .	71
Loosestrife . .	654
Purple . . .	355
Lords and Ladies .	944
Lotus, Common .	266
Slender . . .	267
Lousewort . . .	772
Lovage, Scotch . .	430
Lucern . . .	236
Ludwigia, Marsh .	352
Lungwort . . .	694
Lychnis, Alpine . .	146
Corn . . .	143
Red . . .	142
White . . .	141
Viscid . . .	145
Lymegrass . . .	1208
Lysimachia, Common .	654
Tufted . . .	655
Wood . . .	657
Lythrum, Hyssop .	356
MADDER, Field . .	483
Wild . . .	470
Madwort . . .	710
Maiden-hair . . .	1309
Male Fern . . .	1291
Male Fluellen . .	740
Mallow, Common .	197
Dwarf . . .	196
Marsh . . .	199
Musk . . .	198
Tree . . .	195
Maple, Common .	221
Great . . .	222
Sycamore . .	222
Maram . . .	1188
Maram-grass . .	1158
Marestail . . .	397
Marigold, Bur . .	521
Corn . . .	524
Marsh . . .	24
Marjoram, Wild .	789
Masterwort . . .	437
Matgrass . . .	1207
Matricary, Common .	527
Scentless . .	526
Matweed, Sea . .	1188
May . . .	339
May-lily . . .	1034
Mayweed, Stink . .	528
Maywort . . .	471
Meadow Rue . .	4
Saffron . . .	1059
Sweet . . .	302
Medick, Black . .	237
Bur . . .	240
Lucern . . .	236
Purple . . .	236
Sickle . . .	235
Spotted . . .	239
Toothed . . .	238
Medlar . . .	341
Melick, Mountain .	1253
Wood . . .	1254

	FIG.
Melilot, Common .	241
Field . . .	242
White . .	243
Menziesia, Blue .	636
Mercury, Annual	898
Dog's . .	897
Mertensia, Sea .	695
Meu, Spignel .	432
Mezereon . .	880
Miboria . .	1179
Midsummer-men	361
Mignonette, Cut-leaved	115
Dyer's . .	114
White . .	116
Milfoil . .	533
Spiked or Water	395
Whorled . .	396
Milium, Spreading	1159
Milk Parsley .	436
Milk-thistle . .	558
Milkvetch . .	271
Milkwort, Common	127
Sea . . .	659
Millet-grass . .	1159
Mimulus, Yellow	746
Mint, Bergamot .	784
Corn . . .	786
Horse . .	780
Pepper . .	783
Round-leaved .	781
Spear . .	782
Water . .	784
Whorled . .	785
Mistletoe . .	458
Mithridate Mustard	96
Pepperwort .	103
Mœnchia, Upright .	158
Molinia, Purple .	1252
Moneywort . .	656
Monkshood . .	30
Monotrope . .	648
Moonwort . .	1279
Moscatel . .	461
Moss Campion .	134
Motherwort .	809
Mountain-Ash .	338
Everlasting .	512
Mousetail, Common	8
Mudwort . .	747
Mugwort . .	538
Mullein, Dark .	729
Great . .	726
Hoary . .	731
Moth . .	727
Twiggy . .	728
White . .	730
Muscari, Grape .	1047
Musk Thistle .	559
Mustard, Black .	83
Cultivated .	81
Garlick . .	73
Hedge . .	70
Mithridate .	96
Treacle . .	74
Tower . .	56
White . .	81
Wild . .	82
Myosote, Changing .	703

	FIG.
Early . . .	702
Field . . .	701
Water . . .	699
Wood . . .	700
NAIAD, Grassy .	955
Holly-leaved .	954
Slender . .	953
Narcissus, Daffodil .	1024
Two-flowered .	1025
Navelwort . .	360
Nettle, Common .	905
Hemp . .	807
Roman . .	904
Small . .	903
Nightshade . .	715
Deadly . .	717
Enchanter's .	353
Nipplewort . .	611
Nitgrass, Awned .	1187
None-so-pretty .	387
Nonsuch . .	237
Nottingham Catchfly	137
Nut . . .	915
OAK, British . .	917
Fern . . .	1284
Oat, False . .	1201
Perennial . .	1199
Wild . .	1198
Yellow . .	1200
Œnanth, Common .	423
Fine-leaved .	426
Hemlock . .	425
Parsley . .	424
Old Man's Beard .	1
Ononis Restharrow .	233
Small . .	234
Opium Poppy .	36
Orache, Common .	856
Frosted . .	857
Garden . .	855
Stalked . .	854
Orchis, Bee . .	1013
Bird's-nest .	991
Bog . . .	981
Butterfly . .	1006
Dark-winged .	999
Dwarf . .	999
Early . .	1000
Fen . . .	982
Fly . . .	1015
Fragrant . .	1007
Frog . . .	1010
Green-winged .	997
Lizard . .	1004
Loose . .	1001
Man . . .	1011
Marsh . .	1003
Military . .	998
Musk . .	1012
Purple . .	1000
Pyramidal . .	1005
Spider . .	1014
Spotted . .	1002
Ornithogalum,	
Drooping . .	1042
Spiked . .	1043

	FIG.
Orpine . . .	362
Osier . . .	923
Oxalis, Procumbent .	218
Sorrel . .	217
Oxeye Daisy .	523
Oxlip . . .	651
Oxtongue . .	580
Oxyrea . .	868
Oxytrope, Purple .	273
Yellow . .	272
PADDOCK-PIPES . 1263–1272	
Pæony . . .	32
Paigle . . .	651
Panicum, Cockspur .	1165
Fingered . .	1160
Glabrous . .	1161
Glaucous . .	1163
Green . .	1164
Rough . .	1162
Pansy, Field . .	126
Garden . .	126
Parsley, Bastard Stone	407
Beaked . 444–446	
Bur . . .	450
Common . .	410
Corn . .	411
Fern . .	1285
Fool's . .	427
Hedge . .	448
Milk . .	436
Piert . .	325
Parsnip, Common .	438
Cow . .	439
Water . .	415
Pasque-flower .	5
Pea, Black . .	297
Earth Nut .	292
Everlasting .	293
Marsh . .	294
Meadow . .	291
Rough . .	290
Sea . .	295
Tuberous . .	296
Pearlwort, Alpine .	148
Knotted . .	149
Procumbent .	147
Pear-tree . .	334
Pellitory, Wall .	906
Pennycress, Alpine .	98
Perfoliate . .	97
Penny-royal . .	787
Pennywort . .	360
Marsh . .	398
Peppermint . .	783
Pepper-Saxifrage .	431
Pepperwort, Mithridate	103
Periwinkle, Larger .	672
Lesser . .	673
Persicaria . .	876
Petty Whin . .	231
Phalaris, Canary .	1168
Pheasant's Eye .	7
Phleum, Alpine .	1171
Bœhmer's .	1172
Rough . .	1173
Sand . .	1174
Physosperm, Cornish .	454

	FIG.
Picris, Hawkweed	581
Pignut	443
Pilewort	14
Pillwort, Creeping	1267
Pimpernel, Bastard	662
Bog	661
Common	660
Scarlet	660
Yellow	657
Pimpinel, Common	417
Greater	418
Pine	936
Ground	821
Pink, Cheddar	132
Deptford	130
Maiden	131
Proliferous	129
Sea	826
Pipewort	1082
Plane, Scotch	222
Plantain, Bucks-horn	832
Greater	828
Hoary	829
Ribwort	830
Sea	831
Water	974
Ploughman's Spikenard	517
Plum	298
Poa, Alpine	1249
Annual	1243
Bulbous	1250
Darnel	1242
Flattened	1244
Floating	1237
Hard	1241
Meadow	1245
Procumbent	1240
Reed	1236
Reflexed	1239
Roughish	1246
Sea	1238
Wavy	1248
Wood	1247
Polycarp, Four-leaved	173
Polygonum,	
Amphibious	875
Bistort	874
Climbing	871
Copse	872
Pale	877
Persicaria	876
Sea	870
Slender	879
Viviparous	873
Waterpepper	878
Polypody, Alpine	1283
Beech	1282
Common	1281
Oak	1284
Pondweed, Acute	966
Broad	958
Curly	963
Fennel	968
Horned	956
Long	961
Obtuse	965
Opposite	964
Perfoliate	962

	FIG
Shining	960
Slender	967
Various-leaved	959
Poor man's weather-glass	660
Poplar, Aspen	934
Black	935
Italian	935
White	933
Poppy, Field	37
Horned	44
Long-headed	38
Opium	36
Pale	40
Rough	39
Sea	44
Welsh	41
Potentil, Hoary	316
Marsh	322
Rock	321
Shrubby	319
Spring	317
Strawberry-leaved	313
Prickwood	460
Primrose, Bird's-eye	652
Common	651
Evening	351
Peerless	1025
Privet	671
Prunella	795
Purslane, Sea	154, 853
Water	357
QUAKEGRASS, Common	1234
Lesser	1235
Queen of the Meadows	302
Queen Stock	48
Quilwort, European	1265
Quitch	1213
RADISH, Wild	113
Ragged Robin	144
Ragwort	547
Rampion	621
Round-headed	615
Spiked	616
Ramps	621
Ramsons	1054
Ranunculus, Bulbous	20
Celery-leaved	15
Corn	23
Creeping	18
Figwort	14
Fine-leaved	19
Hairy	21
Ivy	10
Meadow	17
Small-flowered	22
Snaketongue	13
Water	9
Wood	16
Rape	80
Raspberry	307
Rattle, Common	770
Red	771
Reed	1258
Reedmace, Great	939
Lesser	940

	FIG.
Rest-harrow	233
Rib-grass	828-832
Ribwort	830
Roast-beef-plant	1018
Rock Bracken	1285
Rockcress, Alpine	59
Bristol	62
Fringed	60
Glabrous	56
Hairy	58
Northern	63
Thale	61
Tower	57
Rocket	76
Dyer's	114
London	71
Sea	111
Yellow	51
Rock-rose, Common	119
Hoary	118
Spotted	117
White	120
Rœmerea	43
Romulea	1021
Rose-Bay	342
Burnet	329
Dog	332
Downy	330
Field	333
Scotch	329
Roseroot	361
Rowan-tree	338
Rubus, Stone	810
Ruppia, Sea	957
Rupture-wort	835
Rush, Baltic	1063
Capitate	1071
Chestnut	1075
Club	940, 941
Common	1060
Dutch	1275
Dwarf	1070
Flowering	972
Hard	1061
Heath	1068
Highland	1074
Jointed	1064
Obtuse	1065
Round-fruited	1066
Sea	1072
Sharp	1073
Slender	1067
Thread	1062
Toad	1069
Two-flowered	1076
Ryegrass	1215
SAFFRON, Meadow	1059
Sage, Meadow	777
Wild	778
Wood	815
Sainfoin, Common	277
Salad Burnet	327
Sallow	924
Sallow-Thorn	882
Salsify, Meadow	578
Purple	579
Saltwort, Black	659

	FIG			FIG.			FIG.
Prickly	842	Sedge, Sweet	945	Soapwort	133
Samphire, Golden	516	Sedum, English	363	Solanum, Black	716
Marsh	839	Hairy	366	Solomon-seal, Angular	1032
Sea	433	Orpine	362	Common	1031
Sand Leek	1049	Reflexed-leaved	370	Whorled	1030
Sandspurry	171	Rock	369	Sorrel	866
Sandwort, Bog	152	Roseroot	361	Kidney	868
Fine-leaved	153	Tasteless	368	Sheep's	867
Fringed	156	Thick-leaved	364	Wood	217
Three-nerved	157	White	365	Sowbread	653
Thyme-leaved	155	Selaginella, Common	1264	Sowthistle, Common	594
Vernal	151	Self-heal	795	Corn	592
Sanicle, Wood	399	Senebiera, Common	108	Marsh	593
Sauce-alone	73	Lesser	109	Sparganium, Branched	941
Saussurea, Alpine	557	Senecio, Broad-leaved	550	Simple	941
Sawwort	556	Fen	549	Small	943
Saxifrage, Alpine	385	Field	552	Spartina	1205
Brook	383	Groundsel	542	Spear-thistle	526
Burnet	417	Marsh	551	Spearwort, Great	11
Cut-leaved	379	Narrow-leaved	548	Lesser	12
Drooping	382	Ragwort	547	Speedwell, Alpine	752
Golden	389	Squalid	545	Buxbaum's	762
Kidney	388	Viscous	543	Common	754
London-pride	387	Water	546	Fingered	765
Marsh	378	Wood	544	Germander	759
Meadow	381	Service-tree, Wild	337	Ivy	760
Pepper	431	Seseli, Mountain	429	Marsh	757
Purple	376	Sesleria, Blue	1257	Mountain	758
Rue-leaved	384	Setter-wort	27	Procumbent	761
Star	386	Sheep's-bit	614	Rock	751
Tufted	380	Sheep-sorrel	867	Spiked	750
Yellow	377	Shepherd's-needle	441	Thyme-leaved	753
Scabious, Field	496	Purse	102	Vernal	764
Small	495	Weather-glass	660	Wall	763
Scheuchzeria, Marsh	969	Shieldfern, Broad	1293	Water	755
Schœnus, Black	1085	Crested	1292	Spignel meu	432
Scirpus, Bristle	1099	Marsh	1289	Spikenard,	
Clustered	1101	Mountain	1290	Ploughman's	517
Creeping	1094	Prickly	1288	Spindle-tree	224
Few-flowered	1096	Rigid	1294	Spiræa, Willow	301
Floating	1098	Shore weed	833	Spleenwort, Black	1301
Lake	1104	Sibthorpia	748	Common	1299
Many-stalked	1095	Silene, Dwarf	134	Forked	1304
Needle	1092	Night-flowering	140	German	1303
Savi's	1100	Small-flowered	138	Green	1300
Sea	1105	Spanish	136	Lanceolate	1297
Sharp	1102	Striated	139	Rock	1296
Small	1093	Silverweed	320	Sea	1298
Triangular	1103	Simethis, Variegated	1056	Spurge, Broad	887
Tufted	1097	Sison, Hedge	407	Caper	892
Wood	1106	Sisyrinchium,		Dwarf	891
Scorpion grass	699–703	Narrow-leaved	1020	Hairy	889
Scrophularia,		Sium, Broad	415	Irish	883
Balm-leaved	744	Lesser	416	Laurel	881
Knotted	742	Skullcap, Common	796	Leafy	895
Water	743	Lesser	797	Petty	890
Yellow	745	Sloe	298	Portland	893
Scurvy-grass	86	Smallreed, Narrow	1191	Purple	835
Seablite	840, 841	Purple	1190	Sea	894
Sea-buckthorn	882	Wood	1189	Sun	886
Heath	128	Snake root	874	Wood	896
Holly	401	Snakes-head	1037	Spurry, Corn	172
Kale	112	Snakeweed	874	Sandwort	171
Lavender	823	Snapdragon, Great	732	Squill, Autumnal	1045
Milkwort	659	Lesser	733	Bluebell	1046
Pink	826	Sneezewort	532	Spring	1044
Purslane	154	Snowdrop	1026	Squinancywort	482
Rocket	111	Snowflake	1027	Squirrel-tail Grass	1211

	FIG.
Stachys, Field . .	804
Hedge . . .	802
Marsh . . .	803
Star-fruit . . .	977
Star of Bethlehem .	1041
Yellow . . .	1040
Star-thistle . .	576
Starwort, Bog . .	167
Great . . .	170
Lesser . . .	168
Marsh . . .	169
Water . . .	164
Wood . . .	165
Statice, Matted . .	825
Rock . .	824
St. Dabeoc's Heath .	635
St. John's-wort . .	181
St. Patrick's Cabbage	387
Stink May-weed . .	528
Stitchwort . . .	170
Lesser . . .	168
Stock, Common . .	48
Queen . . .	48
Sea . . .	49
Stonecrop . . .	362
Biting . . .	367
Stork's-bill . .	214–216
Strapwort . . .	834
Stratiotes, Water .	980
Strawberry, Wild .	312
-tree . . .	630
Suæda, Herbaceous .	841
Shrubby . .	840
Succory . . .	609
Lamb's . . .	610
Swine's . . .	610
Sulphur-weed . .	435
Sundew, Common .	392
English . . .	394
Oblong . . .	393
Swede . . .	80
Sweet-briar . . .	331
Flag . . .	945
Sedge . . .	945
Swine-cress . . .	108
Sycamore . . .	222
TAMARISC, Common .	176
Tansy . . .	535
Tare . . .	278
Teasel, Fuller's .	492
Small . . .	493
Wild . . .	492
Teesdalia, Common .	99
Thalecress . . .	61
Thalictrum, Alpine .	2
Lesser . .	3
Yellow . .	4
Thistle, Carline .	571
Cotton . . .	570
Creeping . . .	564
Dwarf . . .	569
Marsh . . .	563
Meadow . . .	568
Melancholy . .	566
Milk . . .	558
Musk . . .	559

	FIG.
Scotch . . .	570
Slender . . .	561
Spear . . .	562
Star . . .	576
Tuberous . . .	567
Welted . . .	560
Woolly . . .	565
Thorn-apple . .	713
Thrift, Common	826
Plantain	827
Throw-wax . .	419
Thyme, Basil . .	790
Water . .	978
Wild . . .	788
Tillæa, Mossy . .	359
Timothy-grass . .	1170
Toadflax . . .	734
Bastard . . .	883
Toothwort . .	725
Tormentil . . .	315
Touch-me-not . .	219
Towercress . . .	57
Tower Mustard . .	56
Traveller's Joy . .	1
Treacle Mustard .	74
Trefoil, Bird's-foot .	266
Hare's-foot . .	246
Hop . . .	263
Marsh . . .	683
Trientale, Common .	658
Trigonel, Bird's-foot	244
Trinia, Common . .	408
Triodia, Decumbent .	1255
Trollius, Globe .	25
Tulip, Wild . .	1038
Turnip . . .	80
Tutsan . . .	180
Twayblade, Common	989
Lesser .	990
VACCINIUM, Bog .	627
Valerian, Common .	486
Greek . . .	685
Marsh . . .	485
Pyrenean . . .	487
Red . . .	484
Spur . . .	484
Venus's-comb .	441
Vervein . . .	822
Vetch, Bithynian .	287
Bitter . . .	282
Bush . . .	233
Common . . .	285
Hairy . . .	278
Horse-shoe . .	276
Kidney . . .	268
Milk . . .	271
Slender . . .	279
Spring . . .	286
Tufted . . .	280
Upright . . .	282
Wood . . .	231
Yellow . . .	284
Vetchling, Grass	288
Yellow . .	289
Violet, Dame's . .	69
Dog . . .	125

	FIG.
Hairy . . .	123
Marsh . . .	121
Sand . . .	124
Sweet . . .	122
Water .	649
Wood . . .	125
Viper's Bugloss . .	692
WAKE Robin . .	944
Wallcress . . .	61
Wallflower . . .	50
Wall-Pepper . .	367
Wallrue . . .	1302
Wartcress . . .	108
Watercress, Common .	52
Creeping . . .	53
Great . . .	55
Marsh . . .	54
Water Dropwort . .	423
Fennel . . .	9
Hemlock . . .	403
Lily, White . .	34
Yellow . .	35
Milfoil . . .	905
Parsnip . . .	415
Pepper . . .	177
Plantain . 974, 975,	976
Purslane . . .	357
Soldier . . .	980
Starwort . . .	902
Thyme . . .	978
Violet . . .	649
Waterwort . 177,	178
Waybent . . .	1211
Wayfaring-tree . .	464
Weather glass,	
Poor Man's . .	660
Shepherd's . .	660
Weld . . .	114
Whin . . .	227
Petty . . .	231
White Bottle . .	135
White-rot . . .	398
Whitethorn . . .	339
Whitlow-grass . .	93
Whortleberry . .	626
Red . . .	628
Willow, Almond .	921
Bay . . .	918
Common . . .	920
Crack . . .	919
Creeping . . .	927
Downy . . .	923
Dwarf . . .	932
French . . 342,	921
Goat . . .	924
Golden . . .	920
-herb . .	343–349
Osier . . .	923
Purple . . .	922
Reticulate . . .	931
Rose . . .	922
Round-eared . .	925
Sallow . . .	924
Tea-leaved . .	926
White . . .	920
Whortle . . .	930

8938249R0

Made in the USA
Lexington, KY
15 March 2011